The Barnes SPORTS LIBRARY

ARCHERY
ARCHER'S CRAFT by Hodgkin
ARCHERY by Reichart and Keasey

BADMINTON
WINNING BADMINTON by Davidson and Gustavson

BASEBALL
WINNING BASEBALL by Allen
BASEBALL TECHNIQUES ILLUSTRATED by Allen and Micoleau
DICTIONARY OF BASEBALL by Cummings
HOW TO PITCH by Feller
BASEBALL by Jessee

BASKETBALL
BASKETBALL TECHNIQUES ILLUSTRATED by Anderson and Micoleau
SCIENCE OF COACHING by Bee
DRILLS AND FUNDAMENTALS by Bee
MAN-TO-MAN DEFENSE AND ATTACK by Bee
ZONE DEFENSE AND ATTACK by Bee
BASKETBALL FOR GIRLS by Meissner and Myers
BASKETBALL ILLUSTRATED by Hobson
BASKETBALL by Murphy

BOWLING
BOWLING FOR ALL by Falcaro and Goodman
MODERN BOWLING TECHNIQUES by McMahon and Goodman
DUCK PIN BOWLING by Weinberg
BOWLING by Wilman

FENCING
FENCING by Vince

FISHING
SURF FISHING by Evanoff
HOW TO TIE FLIES by Gregg
BAIT ROD CASTING by Leonard
FLY ROD CASTING by Leonard
BLUEFISHING by Lyman

FOOTBALL
FUNDAMENTAL FOOTBALL by Holgate
OFFENSIVE FOOTBALL (The Belly Series) by Olivar
TOUCH FOOTBALL by Grombach
WINNING FOOTBALL PLAYS by Camerer
SIX-MAN FOOTBALL by Duncan
FOOTBALL by Killinger
FOOTBALL TECHNIQUES ILLUSTRATED by Moore and Micoleau

GOLF
GOLF ILLUSTRATED by Berg and Cox

HANDBALL
HANDBALL by Phillips

HOCKEY
ICE HOCKEY by Jeremiah
FIELD HOCKEY by Lees and Shellenberger

HUNTING
DEER HUNTING by Park

KITES
KITES by Fowler

PHYSICAL CONDITIONING, SELF DEFENSE
SELF DEFENSE by Brown
TUMBLING TECHNIQUES ILLUSTRATED by Burns and Micoleau
DEFEND YOURSELF! by Grover
BOXING by Haislet
JIU-JITSU by Lowell
WEIGHT LIFTING by Murray
PHYSICAL CONDITIONING by Stafford and Duncan
WRESTLING by Gallagher and Peery

RIDING AND ROPING
RIDING SIMPLIFIED by Self
ROPING by Mason

SAILING, BOATING
BOATING—A Beginning Guide by Allen
SKIING ON WATER by Andresen
START 'EM SAILING by Aymar

SKATING
CHAMPIONSHIP FIGURE SKATING by Lussi and Richards

SKIING
POWER SKIING ILLUSTRATED by Micoleau
SKIING by Prager

SOCCER
SOCCER ILLUSTRATED by DiClemente

SOFTBALL
SOFTBALL FOR GIRLS by Mitchell
SOFTBALL by Noren

SWIMMING
SWIMMING by Kiphuth

TENNIS
TENNIS FOR BEGINNERS by Murphy-Murphy
TENNIS MADE EASY by Budge
TABLE TENNIS ILLUSTRATED by Cartland
TENNIS by Jacobs
TENNIS TECHNIQUES ILLUSTRATED by Mace and Micoleau

TRACK AND FIELD
CROSS-COUNTRY TECHNIQUES ILLUSTRATED by Canham and Micoleau
FIELD TECHNIQUES ILLUSTRATED by Canham and Micoleau
TRACK TECHNIQUES ILLUSTRATED by Canham and Micoleau
TRACK AND FIELD by Conger
PRACTICAL TRACK ATHLETICS by Kinzle

VOLLEY BALL
VOLLEY BALL by Laveaga

This library of sports books covers fundamentals, techniques, coaching and playing hints and equipment. Leading coaches and players have written these volumes. Photographs and drawings illustrate techniques, equipment and play.

FIELD HOCKEY

For Players, Coaches, and Umpires

Josephine T. Lees

Former Coach, Rhode Island University

Betty Shellenberger

United States First Team, 1939-1955

THE RONALD PRESS COMPANY • New York

Library of Congress Catalog Card Number: 57-11290
PRINTED IN THE UNITED STATES OF AMERICA

Preface

About fifty years ago field hockey was a new game to Americans. Since that time it has made a place for itself throughout the country. It is played in junior and senior high schools, private schools, colleges, universities, and organized city and sectional clubs. Hockey enthusiasts from many parts of the United States participate in the yearly national tournaments conducted by the United States Field Hockey Association, and touring teams made up of the best players represent the United States in matches played in foreign countries. Not only because of its enthusiastic leaders and its thorough national and sectional organization but also because of the innate appeal of this fast-moving game, hockey has become the most popular outdoor team sport among American girls and women.

Everyone who plays the game acquires a deep personal satisfaction from well-executed strokes and proficiency in her position on the team. A cooperative team spirit and an increased sense of sportsmanship develop in all who participate. The game offers excellent recreational opportunities for young and old, alike. This book is dedicated to those who enjoy the game and who want to learn more about the intricacies of its make-up.

Prepared for player, coach, and umpire, this book covers equipment, individual skills, team tactics, and umpiring techniques and integrates the materials to show the relationship of one to the other. With the aid of photographs the authors tell how to execute each stroke and how to use the stroke in game situations. They mention practice procedures to help the player develop skillful stickwork. Then duties of each of the eleven players on offense and defense are discussed. Special attention is given to forward-line tactics in passing, dodging, and shooting for goal; backfield strategy in marking, backing up, and covering; and goaltending maneuvers in the striking circle. The many diagrams show a "perfect" attack or defense response to a stated game situation. These illustrations help a player visualize her function in relation to her teammates and to her opponents and assist a coach in her explanation of player-movements and teamwork on the field.

No person can be well versed in field hockey unless she understands the umpire's part in the game. The book, therefore, covers the technique of umpiring in detail, from before-game duties, positioning, and signaling, to the umpire's prerogatives in innumerable game situations.

In many ways the field hockey vocabulary is unique. So that the inexperienced and uninitiated will have a ready reference for unfamiliar words and expressions, the book concludes with an extensive glossary of field hockey terms.

One of the authors of the book, Betty Shellenberger, posed for the photographs which illustrate hockey techniques. Appreciation is extended to Doris R. Cholerton, of the Philadelphia Field Hockey Association, who helped the author demonstrate the lunges, right cut, circular tackle, and bully, and who posed for the picture on goaltending; and to John Cholerton for his excellent photography. Lincoln H. Reid drew the diagrams, and the authors are indebted to him for his meticulous care in their preparation.

May E. Parry, National Umpire and Swarthmore College coach, deserves special recognition. She contributed the chapter on Umpiring Technique, and the authors gratefully acknowledge her part in the preparation of this book.

Josephine T. Lees
Betty Shellenberger

Contents

List of Illustrations

Explanation of Symbols

DEFENSIVE TEAM—A. The arrow in the margin of the diagram shows the direction in which the team is playing. The members of the defensive team are represented by encircled capital letters:

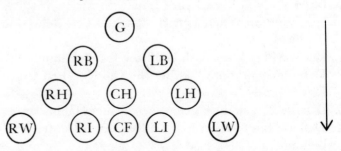

OFFENSIVE TEAM—*b*. The arrow in the margin of the diagram shows the direction in which the team is playing. This team has the ball. The members of the offensive team are represented by lower case letters:

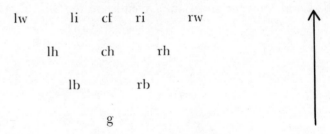

The ball: black dot •
The path of the ball: solid line, with a directional arrow ⟶
The path of the player: broken line, with a directional arrow ⤑

Chapter I

The Game of Field Hockey

The modern game of field hockey originated in England about the middle of the nineteenth century. Centuries previous crooked stick and ball games were popular in Europe, variously called hurley in Ireland, shinty in Scotland, bandy in Wales, hoquet in France; but because the present game rose to its greatest heights of popularity in England, people are inclined to label it an English game.

Until 1887 hockey was the exclusive property of men, being regarded as too rough and dangerous a game for women. But in that year the English ladies adopted the game and organized the first field hockey club in East Molesey. In 1895 the English Ladies' Hockey Association, subsequently called the All-England Women's Hockey Association, was formed. This Association, together with the English men's groups, proceeded to popularize hockey throughout the world.

FIELD HOCKEY IN THE UNITED STATES

Women who enjoy playing, coaching, or umpiring the national amateur sport of field hockey in the United States today owe allegiance to a member of the British College of Physical Education, Miss Constance M. K. Applebee, who figured prominently in the development of the game among Americans. During the summer of 1901 Miss Applebee came to the United States to study anthropometry at Harvard Summer School. One time, in discussing relative merits of British and American women athletes, Miss Applebee said, "An English woman cannot be judged athletically until she has performed in field hockey." Among the group interested in this statement were Harriet I. Ballantine, director of physical education from Vassar College, Dr. R. Tait McKenzie, anatomy professor from McGill University, and Dr. Dudley A. Sargent, the teacher of the course and Director of the Hemenway Gymnasium. Since none had any knowledge of field hockey, Miss Applebee gathered together ice hockey sticks, shinny sticks, and an indoor baseball, lined the concrete courtyard outside the Harvard gymnasium with chalk, and demonstrated the English sport.

That fall, Miss Ballantine invited Miss Applebee to instruct the Vassar College girls in the game. Miss Applebee found twenty-four hockey sticks at

Spaldings in New York (discarded by an Englishman who had unsuccessfully tried to interest American men in field hockey) and arrived at Vassar with this equipment and a cricket ball. Because of the interest exhibited by students and teachers, she repeated her instruction at Wellesley, Radcliffe, Smith, Mt. Holyoke, and Bryn Mawr, where she later became games mistress.

At Bryn Mawr College Miss Applebee taught hockey and stimulated the girls to play and coach the game after their graduation. Miss Catherine Wagner, one of Miss Applebee's pioneers, interested a group in Germantown, and these girls used the cricket pitch at Germantown Cricket Club for their matches. Additional hockey groups appeared and played matches at various cricket clubs in and around Philadelphia. In 1904 four Philadelphia teams united to form the Philadelphia Field Hockey Association. In 1907 the Association boasted eight teams; this group arranged a tournament and competed for a challenge cup. Not long after this organized teams appeared in the vicinity of New York City and as far north as Boston. Because of Miss Applebee's influence, American women aped the English pattern of club and league organization, and such unification has been a real factor in the success and continued popularity of the game. As a result of Miss Applebee's settling in the Philadelphia area, this vicinity became the center of field hockey in the United States.

In 1920, at the instigation of Miss Applebee, a group of Philadelphia players toured England, as guests of the All-England Women's Hockey Association. Needless to mention that the scores of the matches were sadly one-sided; the Americans, however, learned a great deal on this touring trip about style of play, tactics, rules, and ethics. A direct result of the visit was a "drastic" change in the American hockey costume. From six inches from the ground the American players raised their heavy corduroy skirts to the shocking height of eight inches from the ground! The next year a representative English team, sponsored by the Philadelphia Field Hockey Association, played in the Philadelphia area and gave instructional help in several eastern schools and colleges. Within a short span of twenty years—through dedicated interest and organization—field hockey had become a recognized sport for women.

The United States Field Hockey Association, the governing body of women's field hockey, was inaugurated in Philadelphia on January 21, 1922. Mrs. Edward B. Krumbhaar, a prominent Philadelphia player, became the first president, and Helen Ferguson, secretary. From its inception the Association pledged itself to spread and advance the best interests of hockey throughout the United States. It laid plans for uniting the players into clubs and sections, and for standardizing the rules and equipment. In November of that year the USFHA sponsored its first tournament. Four local associations, with a combined membership of twenty-four clubs, entered teams.

At its inauguration meeting the USFHA appointed a committee to seek out English players to help coach club, school, and college teams. Eight players from the All-England Women's Hockey Association responded to the call for assistance and came to the United States to teach hockey in 1922 and 1923. In September of 1922 Miss Applebee started a fall camp for intensive hockey instruction at Mount Pocono, Pennsylvania. Here, for nearly forty years, hockey enthusiasts—teachers and players—have learned to improve their play under the tutelage of Miss Applebee and her hockey staff.

The USFHA, with a membership of more than 150 clubs, works through its eight sectional organizations: Midwest, Northeast, Southeast, Pacific Southwest, Great Lakes, New-Atlantic, Philadelphia, and Mideast. Each section, headed by a chairman, is composed of innumerable local associations. To qualify as a recognized local, the group must have at least three active clubs which must play a minimum of four matches each season. A player must be at least seventeen years of age to play on an association team. The sections conduct tournaments for their locals every year, and at the end of a sectional tournament a selection committee names the section's first and reserve teams from the players of the competing local groups. A National Tournament Committee arranges the annual tournament, where the sectional teams compete. The tournament is usually held at Thanksgiving at a place determined by the USFHA Executive Committee, a local association as hostess. At the national tournament, a Selection Committee of the USFHA names the All-United States First and Reserve Teams which represent the best of hockey in the United States. The first All-United States teams were selected at the national tournament in 1923 and have been named each year since, with the exceptions of the World War II years, 1942-1945, when national tournaments were not scheduled, and 1936, when the 1935 teams participated in the International Conference.

In January, 1924, the All-United States Team made its first official tour, playing in the British Isles and in Paris, France. At the conclusion of the tour the players participated in a hockey conference, held at Merton Abbey near London, March 8, 1924, and attended by representatives of several countries. Planning at this meeting resulted in the formation of the International Federation of Women's Hockey Associations in 1927 in London, with the United States and seven other countries as charter members. The objective of this Federation is to standardize and popularize field hockey among women of all nations through conferences scheduled every three years in different parts of the world. Now the IFWHA includes among its membership Argentina, Australia, Austria, Belgium, England, Holland, India, Ireland, New Zealand, Scotland, South Africa, Spain, Switzerland, United States, and Wales.

The first International Conference was held in Geneva, Switzerland, in 1930, with teams of representative players from the British Isles playing a demonstration game. The United States touring team attended the Federation conference in Copenhagen in 1933; afterwards it toured Denmark, Germany, Holland, and the British Isles; Australia in 1938; British Guiana in

1939; and England, Scotland, and the Netherlands in 1948. The touring team planned to take part in the conference in 1939 in England, but this meeting was cancelled because of unsettled world conditions. Upon resumption of the conference in Johannesburg, South Africa, in 1950, the United States was represented here and after the meetings toured South Africa and Southern Rhodesia. England held the 1953 IFWHA conference at Folkestone. This was one of the most outstanding conferences, attended by eighteen countries. The United States team toured Scotland and the Channel Islands before the conference, and the British Isles directly afterward. Ten countries were represented at the 1956 conference in Sydney, Australia, Canada fielding a team for the first time. The United States team toured Australia, New Zealand, and Fiji after these international matches.

Teams from abroad have played in the United States, competing against the All-United States Team as well as touring and playing local association teams. In 1925 and 1954 the Irish Ladies Hockey Union played here; the English team came in 1928 and 1947; representatives from Scotland visited in 1931 and 1951; and the Welsh Touring Team in 1957. In 1936, when the USFHA sponsored the International Federation matches in Philadelphia, six foreign teams—England, Ireland, Scotland, Wales, Australia, and South Africa—toured the United States before and after the tournament contests.

In addition to sponsoring foreign tours the USFHA, through the work of the Extension Committee, sent touring teams to Ohio and Indiana in 1926; to California, Washington, and Oregon in 1930; to the South in 1936; and to the South and West in 1940. These teams have stimulated interest throughout the United States in the game of field hockey through their demonstration games and by their willingness to help groups in need of instruction and coaching.

Because leaders recognized the fact that good umpiring would promote good play, the USFHA formed an Umpiring Committee as early as 1924. This national committee, together with the sectional and local chairmen, deserves recognition for maintaining the high standards of the game. The Umpiring Committee publishes an Operating Code for Umpiring which clarifies the committee organization and duties and indicates the requirements for national, sectional, and local ratings. The committee interprets the official rules, gives ratings after written examination and practical trials, and advises clubs and schools on rules and umpiring problems. To those umpires who have demonstrated outstanding ability, the USFHA awards a National Umpire rating, which parallels the highest rank for players.

The official rules for field hockey were adopted by the National Division of Girls and Women's Sports, the governing body for standards and playing rules for girls' sports, of the American Association for Health, Physical Education and Recreation. A Field Hockey Committee, composed of appointments from USFHA and the Division, works on hockey policies and procedures. For the Association the Division publishes the *Official Field Hockey*

Guide, which contains the official rules, articles of interest, and national, sectional, and local committees and officers.

To help promote field hockey the USFHA has active committees which assist the work of the parent organization. In addition to the Selection, Umpiring, Extension, and National Tournament Committees previously mentioned, groups take care of situations regarding equipment, insurance, publicity and promotion, and technical service. Committees also work on constitutional questions, membership and honorary membership recommendations, nominations for officers, and sectional problems. The USFHA has an International Federation Women's Hockey Association rules chairman and an international liaison officer. *The Eagle,* the official publication of the Association, appears during the playing season. This journal publishes technical and coaching articles and keeps hockey enthusiasts informed of special events.

In the United States men participate in the game of field hockey in a desultory sort of way. Though organized teams now exist in Westchester County, New York, New York City, Philadelphia, Baltimore, and Washington—and a few groups in other parts of the country—the general impression continues to exist among Americans that field hockey is a woman's game. A men's squad, however, represented the United States in field hockey at the Olympic Games in 1932, 1936, 1948, and 1956. The Field Hockey Association of America was formed in 1930 to control the men's sport, and this Association became affiliated with the American Olympic Association and with the Fédération Internationale de Hockey. The Fédération has a membership of about thirty countries, including the United States. To mention only a few, the leading countries in men's field hockey are India, England, the Netherlands, Germany, and Pakistan, but it is a popular team sport in Australia, Afghanistan, Belgium, Canada, Kenya, Malaya, New Zealand, Singapore, and South Africa.

DESCRIPTION OF THE GAME

Field hockey is a goal game played on a turf field by two teams of eleven players. Each player uses a curved stick to advance a ball toward the opponent's goal, the objective being, through teamwork and strategy, for one team to score more goals than the other. A goal counts one point. The regulation playing time for the game is sixty minutes, with thirty-minute halves and no overtime.

The rectangular field, 90 to 100 yards long by 50 to 60 yards wide, is marked with white lines: those running the length of the field are called side lines; those running across the ends of the field are called goal lines. The field is divided into four parts by lines parallel to the goal lines—the center line crosses the middle; the two 25-yard lines cross 25 yards from the goal lines. Two lines running parallel to the side lines and 5 yards from these lines are designated 5-yard lines; the alley is the space between. The mouth of the goal is 4 yards wide in the center of the goal line. This space is limited by two goalposts and a horizontal crossbar 7 feet from the ground. To outline a scoring area a line is painted 4 yards long, 15 yards from the goal mouth and parallel to it, and continued to the goal line on each side by quarter circles, with radii of 15 yards using the goalposts as centers. The enclosed space and the lines are called the striking circle (Diagram 1, page 10). To score a goal the ball must be hit by an attacking player within this circle and must go across the goal line between the posts and under the crossbar.

The curved wooden stick used to advance the ball has a head which is rounded on its right side and has a flat surface on its left side. Only the flat surface may be used to hit the ball. The drive must be controlled so that no part of the stick raises higher than the hitter's shoulders or else the hitter's team will be penalized. The ball weighs about 5½ ounces, with a cork center and a leather or plastic cover.

Of the eleven players on a team five make up a forward line, three a half-back line, two a fullback combination, and one a goaltender. All players must have stick in hand when they are in a game, may hit and pass the ball in any direction, and may stop the ball with stick, foot, or hand. The goalkeeper is the only player who may kick the ball.

The game starts and restarts after each goal by a bully in the center of the field. To bully, two players stand at opposite sides of a stationary ball and tap the ground and each other's sticks alternately three times, after which each is free to play the ball. If the attackers hit the ball over the goal line without a goal being scored, the game is restarted by a bully on the nearer 25-yard line. If the defenders accidentally hit the ball over the goal line, a corner hit is awarded. For this hit the defenders are required to arrange themselves behind the goal line and the attackers outside the striking circle until one of the attackers drives the ball in from the corner of the field.

If the defenders hit the ball over the goal line intentionally or commit a foul within the striking circle, a penalty corner hit is awarded. The difference between a penalty corner and a corner is that the attacker is permitted to hit the ball out from a point on the goal line ten yards from either goal post, rather than to hit the ball from a point five yards from the corner of the field. In case of other fouls, a free hit is awarded the team opposed to the offender on the spot where the infraction occurred. If the ball goes over the side line it is hand-rolled back into play by a player of the team opposed to the player who last touched the ball before it went out of bounds. On corner hits, free hits, roll-ins, or bullies all players must remain at least five yards away from the hitter or roller until the ball is returned to play.

The offside rule states that a player in her opponents half of the field cannot be ahead of the ball at the time it is hit or rolled in (by a fellow attacker) unless there are three opponents between her and the goal line. Once the ball is hit or rolled, an attacking player can be ahead of it (wings often are). If a player is called for offside the opposing team is awarded a free hit.

No obstruction is permitted in field hockey. A player cannot place her body between the opponent and the ball. Since the sticks are fairly heavy for hard striking, the game could become quite dangerous if the rules permitted a player to defend the ball with the body and to drive, uncontrolled, from both sides of the stick.

Most players wear shin guards to protect their legs and canvas, rubber-cleated shoes on their feet. The goalkeeper wears wide pads and heavy cleated leather shoes.

A regulation game calls for two umpires, one for each half of the field. An important point in this game is that an umpire may refrain from enforcing a penalty when she believes that to enforce it would give an advantage to the offending team.

EQUIPMENT

The choice of equipment plays a very important part in the game of field hockey. Too heavy a stick hinders technique; lack of shin guards lessens confidence; improper shoes cause insecurity of balance; a rough and unkempt field invites injuries. Good equipment is expensive; however, with proper care it lasts for many seasons and is well worth the initial expenditure.

STICK

Most of the better-grade hockey sticks are imported from England. Before choosing a stick the beginner should seek expert advice concerning the proper kind for her individual use. Players vary in height, weight, and size of hand grip; sticks vary accordingly. The experienced player carefully selects a well-balanced stick, flexible enough to allow fine field work, with sufficient weight in the head to permit hard drives.

Manufacturers use ash in the head, a hard wood that withstands the wear and tear of repeated contacts with the ball. To minimize splintering and breaking, a good stick shows a narrow grain running parallel through the blade. A thick head adds to the driving power; nevertheless, when the head is too thick, technique is impaired. Some sticks are constructed with short heads. These require experience and practice to use. Players who are adept in using a short-head stick have quick and neat ball control. The heads of all sticks are spliced to the handle, the spliced region being protected with a vellum collar or white parchment, lute, or surgical binding.

Cane, fitted with parallel or cross-rubber insertions down the center, makes up the body of the handle. Inexpensive sticks with but one insertion lack a spring in the handle and sting the hands when the ball is fielded. For flexibility and resiliency, a stick fitted with treble rubbers is recommended. A handle too thin tends to break easily; one too thick cramps the muscles of the forearm and tightens up the wrist. One which feels comfortable in the grasp, regardless of its width, produces the best results. Handles are bound with string, covered by a colored grip, and attractively trimmed with short lengths of string. If the grip is not the exact size (grips vary from 15 to 18 inches in length) and an amateur puts it on, using a handling tool and glue, it often slips out of position and requires additional tape to hold it in place. Any reinforcement increases the weight of the stick and spoils its balance. Light sticks permit better finesse in strokes. Most players select 18- to 19-ounce sticks.

The height of the individual and the length of her arms determine the length of her stick. Too short a stick necessitates bending over because of the limited reach; too long a stick tends to cause fouling in tackling. As a general rule, if the player stands upright, grasps the stick naturally with the hands together at the top of the handle, and swings the blade easily backward and forward, just cutting the ground with the blade, the stick is a proper length. The most common lengths are 35, 36, 37, and 38 inches.

Blades of new sticks should be wiped off with linseed oil to preserve the wood. Occasionally the treatment should be repeated during the season, making certain that the blade is thoroughly dry before the application. Never use mineral oils on a hockey stick; they soften the blade and reduce its durability. At the end of a season remove the excess dirt with steel wool, rub the blade with beeswax, paint it with shellac or varnish, wrap it in an oily cloth, and store the stick in a cool, dry place. Rubber grips soften, stick together, and rot; handles crack; blades dry out, splinter, and break if sticks remain in a heated compartment.

Pads

All players should wear shin pads to protect their legs from stick and ball injuries. Many defense players shy away from a hard hit and line players hold back, rather than rushing the goal, if their legs are not protected. Light-weight, black canvas pads with cane or reed ribs are cut to cover the instep and padded to protect the ankle bones. By means of two buckles and adjustable elastic straps the shin pads are fastened snugly on the legs; they will not ride if the foot is put through the instep straps. To prevent the buckles from rubbing against each other and tripping the wearer, all fasteners belong on the outside of the legs. If players wear knee socks, strapless pads can be worn inside the socks.

A goalkeeper will not be timid in fielding hard shots if her insteps, ankles, legs, and knees are protected. Canvas goalkeeping pads have side extensions that present a flat front. This type tends to keep the ball from glancing off the pads into the goal. The pads utilize two or three rolls at the knee to insure comfortable bending, and four buckles and straps to keep them firmly in place on the legs. Since the goalkeeper kicks with the side of her foot, kicking pads afford added protection to her ankles and insteps.

Shoes

Experience indicates that the best canvas hockey shoe for long wear, quick starting, and balance is designed with rubber cleats molded to the rubber soles. Those with cemented rubber studs or bars are impractical because the bars rip off during use. Rubber hockey shoes slip on a wet, muddy field; therefore, a player should have among her equipment items thin, supple leather shoes with cleats nailed to the soles.

Sturdy, deep-cleated, box-toed, leather shoes, carefully padded on the instep, aid goalkeeping technique. The shoes should be large enough for the goalkeeper to wear an extra pair of heavy woolen socks and to insert pieces of sponge rubber under the kicking surfaces to absorb the shock.

COSTUME

Uniforms that allow for complete freedom of movement, such as tunics or shorts and blouses, are recommended. Sweat pants and shirts help players to warm up when the weather is very cold. Wool socks keep the feet warm, absorb perspiration, and act as a cushion in the shoe; cotton socks rub and become damp and blister the feet. Players should not wear colored socks because the dye in the sock may irritate a blistered or cut foot.

BALL

The official match-hockey ball has a cork and spring center and a stitched or seamed leather or plastic cover. It weighs 5½ to 5¾ ounces and is waterproof and coated with white enamel. Some leather covers harden and crack if stored in a dry place; so it is best to purchase fresh balls for each season. After use, the ball loses the enamel and needs a fresh coat of white paint before the next practice. Because match balls are expensive, coaches buy composition cork balls for stick practice. The fact that cork balls chip easily makes them unusable for scrimmage because they are rough and liable to injure the players.

FIELD

The field lines up easily with a marker, prepared lime, and string year after year, if, at the initial layout of the dimensions, permanent 8-inch iron stubs are driven flush with the ground at essential points—that is, the corners (4 stubs), the center line on the side lines (2), the 25-yard lines on the side lines (4), and 15 yards out from each goalpost on the goal lines (4). With each goalpost as the center and a 15-yard piece of heavy cord as a radius, the two quarter circles for the striking area can readily be inscribed and joined by a straight line parallel to the goal line, using a brush and flat white paint rather than a line marker with lime. Use paint for drawing the line across the mouth of the goal. Paint for circle and goal lines last longer than lime and is discernible from a greater distance.

Use paint or lime to indicate the points on the goal and side lines where the ball is placed for corner hits. For ordinary corners eight spots should be marked—5 yards from each corner of the field on the goal lines and the side lines. For penalty corners, four spots should be painted, two on each goal line 10 yards out from the nearer goal post. Diagram 1 (page 10) shows the

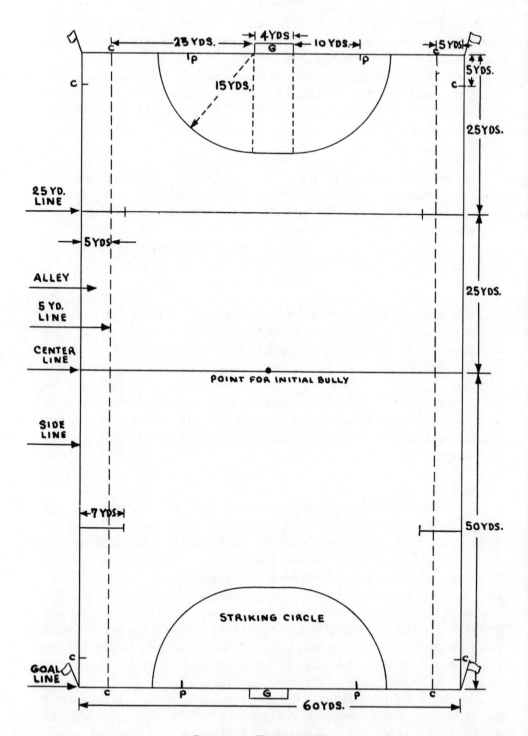

DIAGRAM 1. *The hockey field.*

places from which these corner hits may be taken as well as other line markings for the regulation field. On the diagram, "c" shows the places for eight
markings for the corners and "p" indicates the spots for the four markings for
the penalty corners.

Use lime for marking the 25-yard line. On fields which are less than 100
yards long (regulation length) extend these 25-yard lines across the width of
the field. On a regulation field or one used by experienced players these 25-
yard lines may be suggested by short lines extending in from the side lines a
distance of about 7 yards. Both ways of marking the 25-yard line are shown
in Diagram 1.

Flagposts about 4 feet high may be placed at each corner of the field to
help players, umpires, and spectators locate the four corners readily.

The regulation field for men's field hockey has an alley 7 yards wide (see
markings on lower half of the field on the opposite page) and a radius of 16
yards for the striking circle. Corner hits are taken on a spot 7 yards from the
corner, as contrasted to 5 yards for the girls' game. Other than these few differ-
ences in field markings, both men and women play a similar game.

Goal Cage

Three 2-by 3-inch beams—one for the crossbar, 12 feet long, and two
for the posts, 7 feet long—of seasoned timber, coated several times with outside white paint, make up the front of the cage. Cord or wire nets fasten the
two front posts and crossbar to any kind of painted rear posts and crossbar 4
to 6 feet back and to the ground in order to enclose the entire space. Every-
thing connected with the cage is inconspicuous, except the white front posts
and crossbar.

Chapter II

Strokes, Tackles, and Stops

The game of field hockey demands a knowledge of the timing and control of various strokes in fielding, passing, clearing, shooting, and tackling. Experienced line and backfield players alike uncover opportunities to use every stroke; certain strokes are more effective used by players in certain positions. Rarely do coaches emphasize plays and tactics for team play unless their players handle the ball and stick well. Skillful technique results from careful and constant individual and team practice and adds to both players' and spectators' enjoyment of the game.

Before they can learn any stroke, players must know how to carry the stick, because practically every stroke is initiated from the stick-carry position: the position of readiness. In this two-hand carry the left hand grasps the handle of the stick near the top, back of the hand facing forward; the right hand grips near the splicing, palm facing forward. As the player runs with the stick, her elbows bend comfortably, and her stick swings easily with the motion of running. Never should she swing the top of the handle as high as her shoulders because she is likely to be called for fouling (making "sticks") when she changes to a stroke. Whenever anticipating a tackle, an interception, or a pass, she drops the blade of the stick toward the ground, slipping the right hand to the position on the handle her stroke requires.

In making a long run some players feel that they cover ground faster if they carry the stick in either the left or right hand, rather than across the body in both hands. In this variation of the carry they balance the stick by grasping in the middle of the handle and run with the stick out to their side. Undoubtedly this permits greater speed in running, but this style handicaps a player when she trys to get both hands on the stick again, running at top speed. If she can manage to do this quickly, then the one-handed carry is valuable when a long run is anticipated. As a general practice, though, the two-handed carry permits a safer, surer, and not much slower method of changing to a stroke.

STROKES

An experienced player has a repertory of eleven different strokes. Each of these is described in this section, and the majority are pictured. After the fundamental skills are learned, practice all strokes under game situations. Only by using various strokes in a fast game can any player become proficient in this game of continuous activity.

DRIBBLE

Good technique in the manipulation of the stick and ball depends upon the foundation stroke, the dribble. Positions of the hands on the stick for the push, flick, drive, and stick stop are but slight modifications of the manner of dribbling. Strength in wrists and arms, control of the ball in propelling and passing, practice in running and conditioning of the body depend upon efficiency in dribbling. Practice in driving, for instance, will aid little in improving endurance for a regulation game. The dribble demands first attention.

FIGURE 1. *Dribble*—Side view, showing stick in perpendicular position about to tap ball.

If a player lays a hockey stick on the ground, perpendicular to her body and with the flat of the blade facing upward, then reaches over with her left hand to take a firm hold close to the top of the handle, straightens up and holds the stick parallel to her body, rounded side next to her legs, she will have her left hand placed correctly for the dribble. In other words, to derive full benefit from the wrist, the player must have the back of her hand facing forward with the grip at the top of the handle. Any other hold, especially one with the back of the wrist toward the body, impedes the movement of the left wrist and wastes time by necessitating a shift of grip to change to another stroke. Some girls point the index finger down the handle of the stick

FIGURE 2. *Dribble*—Front view, showing position of hands on the stick and of stick and ball in front and to the right of the right foot.

toward the ground rather than curving it around the handle, hindering the left-wrist motion and inviting injury to the finger. Others grasp the handle several inches from the top, blocking the action of the left wrist and causing the player to dribble in a bent position.

The right hand grasps the handle several inches below the left, with the palm facing forward. This hand steadies the stick in the backward and forward motion of the left wrist in advancing the ball. As players become proficient in form and speed, the left and right hands separate only 3 or 4 inches and the body becomes more erect. Neither hand holds the club tightly; rather, for efficiency in ball control, both hands and arms relax to promote flexibility of the wrists and arms. To allow freedom in activity the left elbow bends slightly to hold the wrists, elbows, arms, and stick away from the body, and to permit the stick to meet the ball almost at a perpendicular. Otherwise, a player cramps her method of dribbling and shifting grips and may injure herself by running onto the handle of her stick.

Whether a player dribbles loosely or closely, a series of hits or taps supplied by the backward and forward motion of the wrist propels the ball ahead, outside the right foot. Beginners should run with short, quick steps and tap the ball when the right foot is ahead.

To consider steps between hits seems awkward at first; and always to tap the ball when the weight is ahead on the right foot involves a shortening or lengthening of stride. A controlled, rhythmical dribble results, though, and with it an ability to change the length of a stride rapidly. A quick and agile player knows how to shift her weight in a split second. Advanced dribblers are almost automatic in their ball-carrying and their tap occurs from either foot.

Inners and center forward keep the ball about a yard from the body and dribble with their stick close to the ball. This permits their passing at any moment and provides less chance for the ball to be taken away. Unless they diligently practice to perfect a close dribble they will kick or overrun the ball more often than they will hit it.

When a forward breaks through a defense and sees a wide-open area ahead, she hits the ball and runs up to it instead of keeping it close to her stick. This hit-and-run dribble, or loose dribble, allows wings, especially, to break away if no one is in the alley or near enough to tackle. Other forwards utilize the loose dribble when they have a clear field before them.

Every player who drives, flicks, or pushes to the right from a dribble, turns with the ball before she passes. To *turn with a ball,* the dribbler has the ball close to her stick in order to shift her position in such a manner that the ball is opposite and away from her right foot (rather than ahead of it), that her feet are ahead of the ball and stick, and that her shoulders are at right angles to the ball, left shoulder leading. If left wing, instead of turning with the ball to place it advantageously for a pass, runs with her left shoulder ahead and actually strokes or spins the ball out to her right side to propel it down the field, she gains a decided advantage in being able to center the ball to her right at full speed. To use this style of dribbling, left wing must always be ahead of the ball to tap or stroke it. An excellent place for practice of the "stroking" dribble is the circle of the striking area. To use this dribble along the circle from right to left, the dribbler runs inside the circle, with the left shoulder leading and the ball slightly behind the right foot on the white curve; from left to right, the player runs outside the circle with the ball behind the right foot on the painted curve.

Each one who dribbles glances up often to take in everyone's position. Only training and experience teach the dribbler the psychological moment to get rid of the ball. Practice proves to her that she is encumbered with a ball; though she propels it at top speed, a fast opponent can overtake her and rob her of the ball when she carries it too long. Also, though a dribbler sees a considerable distance between herself and an opponent, when they run toward each other, she fumbles invariably and loses the ball to an oncoming tackler until she realizes she must time her pass or dodge when her opponent is still several yards away. Therefore, good judgment of the potentialities of

FIGURE 3. *Push*—Start of the stroke: hands apart and stick bent slightly toward the player as it moves against the ball along the ground.

an opponent and accurate timing of passes are prerequisites to skillful dribbling and passing.

Propelling the ball up and down the field with the side or alley line as a
guide helps a player to control the direction of both the loose and close dribble.
For concentrated practice in dribbling closely, carry the ball around ob-
stacles set in a straight line and at least 5 yards apart, or dribble the ball
around the striking circle. Work in pairs to learn to receive the ball from the
right, left, or rear while running and carry the ball ahead with the dribble.
Always maintain a relaxed grip and practice at top speed.

Push

More than any other stroke, the push is employed for short-distance passing. If a player dribbles closely, it can be performed at any moment forward,
sideward, or backward. A quick and easy pass, it is used with little danger of
obstruction, is easily fielded by the receiver, and may be executed on the
run. The direction of the pass can be disguised until the ball is hit. Like the
flick and the scoop, the push is directed to the right more often because it is
easier to use the left drive for passes to the left.

Since the ball is close to the feet at the time of the pass, the push is not a
reaching stroke. The left hand maintains the grasp described for the dribble;
the right hand moves 7 or 8 inches down the stick. As the flat side of the
stick touches the ball, with the top of the handle slightly farther away from
the body than the blade (left elbow bent in front of the body), the right hand
pushes the ball away. No backswing is involved. The right hand scrapes the
stick along the ground in the direction of the pass and acts as a guide to prevent the stick from rising; a slight pull back with the left hand, a straighten-
ing of the right arm, and tightening up of both wrists as the flat of the blade
faces up check the stroke. Since the push starts off the right foot with the
body weight thrown onto the right leg, the left leg follows through at the end
of the stroke.

To use the push for a square pass the ball must be outside the right foot;
for a back pass, the ball must be behind the feet and the shoulders turned
around toward it.

When the technicalities of the push stroke have been studied, practice it
in pairs, preceding the pass with a dribble. Only when players can execute it
both to the stick and nonstick side of the opponent, and can perform it while
on a run, is the push effective.

Flick

Every hockey player uses the flick, a right or left pass that raises the ball
off the ground. Forwards employ this stroke in the striking circle because
goalers are helpless to field it with any degree of accuracy; backs use it to
clear the ball to the sides.

With a relaxed wrist, the left hand grasps the top of the handle in the manner of the dribble; the right hand holds the stick several inches down the handle. The right knee bends more than the left, and the weight is forward on the right foot as a sharp downward push of the left wrist, and an extra bending of the right wrist lift the blade and raise the ball from the ground. At the end of the stroke the blade faces up.

Unlike the push, the flick is a reaching stroke—the ball is far from the foot and the player bends and extends her reach. The top of the handle of the stick is not necessarily farther from the body than the blade; the left foot does not follow through.

Always practice the flick when the ball and player are in motion, to make certain of control and timing. The flick and push are useful in practicing the

FIGURE 4. *Flick*—Position of the stick at the start of the stroke, just before it twists to the right around the ball to give it momentum with a slight spin.

triangular pass (Diagram 5); each one, though, requires different timing. In a circle of players one girl in the center passes with a push or flick to each individual in the group who returns the pass to the center. Speed up the passing and every person benefits in fielding balls, returning balls, pushing, and flicking. Practice in threes—a dribbler drawing out an oncoming tackler and pushing or flicking to a partner on the nonstick side of the tackler—to assist girls in timing their passes accurately.

SCOOP

The scoop stroke is a lifting stroke, particularly effective as a pass to the right or diagonally forward to the right, as a dodge forward over an opponent's stick, or as a shot for goal. Though the ball may be raised high (it will not travel fast enough to injure a player) it covers the distance faster if it is closer to the ground, and the user is less likely to make sticks.

FIGURE 5. *Scoop*—Start of the stroke: stick laid well back just prior to lifting the ball.

The left hand holds the stick in the manner of the dribble; the right hand, as the stick is laid back, grasps just above the splicing, thumb on top. Both elbows bend slightly; the left elbow, wrist, and stick almost form a straight line. To be out of the way of the body, the top of the handle is held out in front of the player's left leg. With this position there is no danger of her running onto the handle and hurting herself if the blade is jabbed at the ground.

The ball is about a yard in front of the player to the right of her right foot when the body leans forward and the arms extend. Both legs bend, the right more than the left because of the weight. As the tip of the stick is placed under the ball there is a deeper bending of both knees; as the ball is lifted, the knees straighten and the left leg follows through. A common error is to try to scoop with the curve of the blade rather than the tip; this fails to lift the ball any distance.

The left hand steadies the stick and exerts a downward pressure; simultaneously, the right wrist and hand move in a forward-upward direction that scoops the ball into the air. Too much wrist action raises the ball too high. At the completion of the stroke the blade is about knee high. When a player realizes the scoop is a shoveling or a lifting stroke, she will see the advantage of keeping her weight forward and laying her stick back toward the ground.

The scoop as a surprise stroke throws an attacker off balance. Left inner and left wing utilize it to get the ball over their opponent's stick when their bodies or sticks are in a poor position for a pass to the right; left inner finds it valuable in the striking circle; all players employ it to pass to a teammate or to dodge by an opponent and find it to be an exceptional wet-weather stroke.

Scooping on the run from a dribble and scooping on the run for goal may be practiced individually. Utilize pairs to scoop and dodge, and threes —a defender and two attackers—to scoop and pass on the run in order that accurate timing can be assured.

Reverse

Players use the reverse stroke as a pass to the right or back, or as a a dodge. Left wing, to throw off-balance a tackler running diagonally toward her, reverses her stick and pulls the ball back to her right, so that she can step back with her right foot and drive to the right. If she finds herself being tackled near the goal line, the trick of pulling the ball back works well. In trying to save the ball from going over the goal line, left inner uses the reverse stroke to pass back to her center forward (Diagram 4). All players employ the reverse stroke as a dodge (Diagram 8). Left halfback and left fullback, in a hurry to overtake a hardhit ball, reverse their sticks to drive the ball back to a teammate before they check their speed and change their direction. If attackers remember never to reach out to the left or behind for the ball with a reversed stick, they will not foul by obstructing with their shoulders. Coaches teach the right drive rather than the reverse stroke as a pass to the right, not only because players often obstruct when they use a reversed stick, but also because players must have strong wrists and an extremely good eye to hit the ball with the toe of the stick.

With the hands close together, the left hand grasping the handle as described in the drive, the player turns the handle in her grip so that the toe of the stick points down. She makes certain that her hands are in the same position after she reverses her stick as they were before. Beginners sometimes reverse their sticks by crossing their wrists rather than by turning the handle in the grasp; when this is the case, they are too cramped to pass the ball.

The force for a pass is obtained mainly from the wrists and forearms, as both the backswing and follow-through are short. When the toe of the stick meets the ball, the direction of the right shoulder determines the direction of the pass.

To practice turning the handle in the grasp, alternate a dribble tap with a reverse-stroke hit to propel the ball down the field. Practice in twos to try the reverse-stroke dodge—one to dodge and one to tackle; using the hit-and-run dribble, practice the pass back to a teammate with a reversed stick or a pull-back with the reverse to place the ball for a drive to the right.

DRIVE

The drive is the stroke that is used for hard clearing passes (Diagram 6); long, diagonal passes (Diagram 5) and centering passes (Diagram 2); hard shots for the goal from the edge of the circle (Diagram 7); short passes to the left; and the majority of free hits. The left drive directs the ball to the left when either foot leads and carries the weight of the body; the right drive sends the ball to the right when the right foot is ahead and carrying the weight. Of the two the left is the stronger and more widely used stroke. Both are performed at full speed; the left is an excellent stroke for a free hit. Players take aim before the backswing and keep their eyes on the ball until they hit.

When any player reaches far out from her body to drive, she lays the blade too far back and fouls by slicing or undercutting the ball.

If forwards in the striking circle use a hard, quick drive for goal with little backswing they may cause defense players to be thrown off on their timing. A short backswing always gives the user the advantage.

Left Drive. To hold the stick properly for this drive a player grasps the handle with her left hand at the top, just as though she were shaking hands with the stick, and then places her right hand as close as possible below the left to add force to the hit. Stand beginners up straight and instruct them to relax their arms and swing their sticks from side to side in the manner of a pendulum. In becoming used to the motion of the stroke and without being too conscious of her arms, a player discovers that her right elbow bends slightly in the backswing while the left remains almost straight; both arms are practically straight in the forward swing.

To drive from a standing position, a player assumes a comfortable stance, with the ball nearer her left foot than her right, and a foot or more ahead of her toes. She faces the ball, pointing her left shoulder toward the direction she wants the ball to go. In the backswing, with the weight on her right foot, the lift of her stick should be in line with the ball to meet it squarely as the stick swings forward. The body weight is behind the shot and moves with the swing from the right to the left foot. In following through, her arms and stick straighten out toward the point of aim and her hands grasp the stick firmly in order to tighten the wrists to prevent the blade from rising high, and her shoulders are over the left foot.

To practice the fundamentals of the stroke two girls stand a short distance

FIGURE 6. *Left drive*—Beginning of the forward swing: ball ahead of the player. Notice the short backswing.

apart and drive toward each other, each fielding the other's hit with her stick. Gradually increase the distance between, until the drive from a stand will travel at least 25 yards.

The left drive, when executed from a run, starts from either foot and may be practiced from a dribble or a slow pass. All forwards practice dribbling at top speed to the edge of the circle, driving to the corners of the goal off whichever foot crosses the circle first, and rushing the hit. Whether or not the goalkeeper is there, forwards rush their drives so they will not form the habit of checking their progress rather than following through.

Right Drive. Left inner and left wing center the ball and shoot for goal with the right drive, center forward and center halfback distribute the play with left and right drives, right inner and right halfback feed their own righ⁺

FIGURE 7. *Right drive*—Beginning of the forward swing: ball to the rear and right of the player. The body twists to make this drive following a short backswing.

wing with this drive, and right fullback and goaler clear from the mouth of the goal with it. Often, when the direction of the pass is from left to right, players shift their feet around to the right by means of a step and a hop, so that they can pass to the right with the left drive. This wastes seconds, and the better players learn to drive with the ball outside or even a little behind the right foot, checking their weight on the right foot during the backward and forward swing. Only when stick meets ball does the left leg follow through. The body twists from the waist; the right shoulder drops, and the left shoulder points toward the line of the intended pass. To be certain the ball goes to the right, the player swings her stick behind her legs. This stroke is not too easily controlled, and "sticks" occurs on the forward swing unless the wrists tighten up considerably.

In an oblique position and far apart, practice in twos, relaying the ball back and forth with a short dribble and a right drive. To practice correctly players move continually in a circle, because one always has to run into position to receive the other's drive. Also, practice in pairs—one dribbling and diagonally passing the ball with the drive; the other receiving the pass, dribbling, and returning the ball with the drive. Thus players utilize both the left and the right drive in motion and afford themselves experience in picking up passes. To assist in timing the drive, practice in twos—one as tackler, the other as dribbler and driver.

TACKLING STROKES

Defense strokes for experienced players—the left- and right-hand lunges, the right cut, and the job—are reaching strokes used in tackling and are difficult to master. Not one of them affords the player complete control of the ball; all hinder the ball-carrier in her progress down the field.

Left-hand Lunge. To players tackling back on the stick side of their opponents, the left-hand lunge is of particular value. To block the ball with this lunge the user should be abreast but not too near her antagonist. From a stick-carry position the tackler lunges forward left, bending her left knee, throwing her weight forward on her left foot, and fully extending her right leg behind. Simultaneously she throws her stick downward across her body with the right hand. Just before the face of the blade meets the ball squarely, she releases the right hand and flings it backward to assist the right leg in balancing the body. As the stick makes contact with the ball, the blade is close to the ground, the stick and left arm are in a straight line, and the wrists lock to avoid a follow-through. To afford a greater leverage the left thumb may be down the stick. This permits more mobility but less control of the stick.

If the lunger runs too close to her opponent, the left arm and shoulder are cramped and the player lacks reach and strength. When the weight is too far forward and the tackler fumbles a lunge, she finds it difficult to regain her balance to make another attempt. Much better than aiming directly at the ball, a player should brush the stick along the ground a little way ahead of the ball. In doing this she may have a chance to field the ball if her opponent tries to pass or if her lunge is not timed exactly. The stick must be kept in contact with the ball until the lunger can get both hands again on the stick to use a stronger tackle. If the blade turns up rather than faces the ball squarely, an undercut results. Obviously, the left-hand lunge must be well controlled to avoid tripping up or hitting the legs or stick of the ball-carrier. Anyone who uses the lunge as a dodge must control the strength of her hit in order not to send the ball out of her own reach.

If the ball-carrier dribbles closely, the tackler blocks the dribble with a lunge in a backward direction. Lunging on a line with the ball minimizes chances of hitting the opponent's stick. She either drives the ball free in the field or catches it between her and her opponent's stick. If the ball is hit free, the dribbler generally overruns the tackle; the defender checks her speed, reverses her direction, and picks up the ball with two hands on her stick. Rather than overruning the ball, the dribbler may stop as her tackler lunges and the ball may be caught between both sticks. If so, the tackler holds her blade against the ball, follows through with her right foot to get in front of the

FIGURE 8. *Left-hand lunge*—Player in dark tunic reaching from behind the ball-carrier to place the stick, held in the left hand, just in front of the ball.

ball, places her right hand halfway down the handle and, with a quick upward movement, lifts the ball over her opponent's stick.

If the ball is dribbled loosely, the lunger may hit it to the side, check her speed, and run behind her opponent to regain the ball. The defender must be careful not to obstruct her opponent by running in front of her. Often, though, the hit travels far enough for the defense's teammate to pick up the ball and the lunger is relieved of the chance of obstructing.

Well-trained players apply the left-hand lunge as a dodge to the left, the user sidestepping in the same direction. This occurs when the ball is equidistant from two opponents (Diagram 8), or when the ball is being dribbled loosely. The lunger has a longer reach than an opponent who uses a two-handed stroke; therefore, a left-hand lunge rather than a straightforward tackle surprises an opponent.

To right wing or right halfback, in attack, the lunge is of value to keep a diagonal pass from going over the side line. Backfield players use it as a hit to the left or employ it to hurry a free hit, so that no opponent has time to mark. It is occasionally used as a shot for goal, when a forward dashes diagonally across the goal mouth to save the ball from going over the goal line and lunges backward toward the mouth of the goal. A lunge is used by defense members to stop a diagonal hit from going over the goal line. In any of these situations the lunge is worthless unless players with good judgment and strong left wrists have perfect timing and exceptional ball control. Concentrate first to perfect the lunge as an overtaking tackle; then try it in some of the instances mentioned above.

Left-handed persons have little difficulty with the left-hand lunge. They are of more value to a team in right wing, right halfback, or right fullback positions, where the left-hand lunge is by far the best overtaking stroke, and where any lunge, pass, or dodge, in attack, will be sent necessarily toward midfield.

In practice, run and lunge at a motionless ball first to measure the distance a player can be from the ball. Then practice in pairs, one dribbling the ball and one overtaking with the lunge. Use the hit-and-run dribble and lunge at a moving ball; attempt to overtake a hard hit ahead and lunge to direct the ball to the side. Have a partner set up the direction of the drives and passes in order to practice control in timing.

Right-hand Lunge. A weak and uncertain stroke, the right-hand lunge is employed only as a last resort. Left halfback and left fullback, who are not in a position to execute a circular tackle, find it imperative to lunge with the right hand. To be of more use to a team, these two players must tackle back on the opponent's nonstick side, since a tackle on the stick side often results in the tackler's setting up a pass to the opponent's teammate in the center of the field or permits the opponent to pass to her center forward. The right-hand lunge is similar to the left stroke only in that it is a one-handed over-

taking stroke; it is not so effective, since the user reverses her stick to lunge
on the nonstick side.

From the stick-carry position a player shifts her stick in the grasp, toe
toward the ground (reversed stick), and places her right hand 3 or 4 inches
from the top of the handle. As she lunges forward with the right foot, her
left hand grasps below the right. Following a short backswing, the player
throws the stick at the ball with her left hand; then she flings the left arm
backward to assist the left leg in the maintenance of balance. The wrist immediately tightens up as the stick taps the ball. Since only the tip of the
blade meets the ball, the right-hand lunge requires exceptional accuracy and
timing. A far better way to overtake and tackle is to run slightly ahead of
the dribbler and utilize the circular tackle (page 31).

FIGURE 9. *Right-hand lunge*—Player in dark tunic, with reversed stick in right hand, about to
contact the ball with the toe of the stick, held in reverse in right hand.

Practice the right-hand lunge in pairs. During individual practice make certain that players do not substitute a badly executed reversed-stick stroke for the reversed-stick lunge.

Right Cut. Though a two-handed stroke, the right cut is a reversed-stick stroke which does not permit control of the ball. Left halfback and left fullback use it when they are about on line with and overtaking an opponent who is dribbling closely.

The tackler uses the reversed-stick grasp and reaches across her opponent for the ball. With the weight on her right foot, she hits the ball with a short, quick tap, firmly gripping the stick to check the stroke, and immediately withdraws the stick to avoid tripping the opponent. Just before the time of contact, the player lifts her stick back and drops her wrists slightly, making certain not to bend her elbows, so that when the stick meets the ball it is not held exactly in a straight line with the arms.

The tackler must be careful not to touch or obstruct her opponent, or hit her opponent's stick before contacting the ball. Unless the tackler allows her opponent time to overrun, she will not be able to play the ball without obstructing. After the tackle, she changes to a dribble or a drive grip. Once she regains the ball she passes it immediately, because the opponent who has checked her progress may spin around and retaliate with a left-hand lunge.

Coaches notice that a weak, cramped stroke results when players twist their wrists to reverse the blade for the right cut, instead of shifting the stick in the grip as they do for the reverse stroke.

Practice this stroke in pairs, the tackler overtaking the dribbler on the nonstick side. Practicing the right cut is valueless unless players shift quickly to regain and clear the ball.

Job. The job, a one-handed stroke performed with the right or left hand, is a poke or thrust at the ball. A player lays the blade back and holds the stick at the end of the handle, wrist on top. She lunges forward, stick and arm in a straight line for strength, and reaches for the ball with the flat of the stick. Care is taken not to lay the blade too far back, or the job will be of no avail; instead of the ball's being pushed away it will roll over the user's stick.

A job is useful when a straightforward tackle is impossible against an oncoming loose dribbler. When an opponent dribbles loosely, players shove the ball just as the opponent's stick is off it. Holding the stick in the right hand, players, especially forwards, thrust the ball over their opponent's stick and quickly regain it. When two players are running for the ball, one jabs it out of her opponent's reach. Without moving out of her position in the striking circle, center halfback can jab at an opposing inner's ball and spoil her shot for goal.

On a tackle back to the nonstick side, the left-hand job, though not permitting a long reach, keeps the right shoulder back and lessens the chances

FIGURE 10. *Right cut*—Player in dark tunic, with firm hold on reversed stick and slightly ahead of ball-carrier, contacts the ball with the toe of the stick.

FIGURE 11. *Job*—Player reaching for the ball, left hand firmly gripping the stick.

of obstructing; on a tackle back on the stick side, the right-hand job serves a similar purpose. Since the job only spoils a stroke, the user in a tackle-back situation follows immediately with a circular tackle to gain control of the ball.

Practice the spoil stroke with a partner who dribbles loosely, tackling back on the stick and nonstick sides.

TACKLES

Good players never hesitate to run forward to attack (tackle) the opponent who has the ball. No matter that the tackler fails to get possession of the ball. The object is to force the ball-carrier to pass the ball, giving the tackler's teammate an opportunity to intercept the pass.

STRAIGHTFORWARD TACKLE

To tackle, a player goes straight toward the ball rather than approach it on an angle, puts her stick forward to the ground about 10 feet before she expects to meet the ball, and holds her hands well apart on the stick for control. Experienced players keep their hands closer together and their stick out in front to increase their reach, though it is difficult to control the placement of the ball this way. The tackler's feet are apart and her weight is on the forward or right foot. As a straightforward tackle is anticipated, the player glues her eyes on the ball and slipsteps quickly to the right (or left) to keep in direct line with it. She pushes the stick against the ball, throwing her weight forward to add force. Players find it easy to tackle if an opponent dribbles loosely or if she loses control of the ball.

OVERTAKING TACKLE

Advanced players are quick to overtake an opponent when their team has lost the ball to the opponent. They tackle back on the inside of the carrier when she approaches the 25-yard line area to keep between her and the goal and to prevent her from passing in. Naturally, this means that the left halfback and the left fullback must tackle on the nonstick side of the ball-carrier. They must be up with the opponent or even a little ahead of her. In other areas of the field it is easier to tackle back on the stick side—first, to avoid a collision; second, to prevent fouling; third, to permit the use of different strokes. A successful tackler employs the left-hand lunge and the job with the right hand when on the stick side; the right-hand lunge, the right cut, the job with the left hand, and the circular tackle, when on the nonstick side. Often a player can move across the field a short distance and intercept a pass before it can reach its intended destination. This may be a disadvantageous practice, though, because if the intercepter misses and she is left behind, the defense players have to shift positions in the field to cover the hole in the defense setup. Anyone not involved in the tackle should anticipate a pass to the left, because generally the tackler overtakes on the stick side, forcing the dribbler to drive to the left. After a successful tackle, use a dodge or short dribble to shake an opponent, then follow immediately with a hard drive to a teammate.

CIRCULAR TACKLE

The circular tackle is an overtaking tackle that includes pushing the ball forward and dribbling it around an opponent in a semicircle. Better still, a player taps it or jabs it to the side, waits for the opponent to overrun, and then circles to pick up the ball. This tackle is performed to the right. The circular tackle gives the user more control of the ball, but it is harder to execute it because the tackler, to initiate it, must be a little ahead of the ball-carrier. As the tackle is performed, the player's body does not follow her stick; it swings around the stick.

FIGURE 12. *Circular tackle*—Player in dark tunic making first contact with the ball. She continues around to the right.

STOPS

Players discover that the position of the hands on the stick in stopping the ball is a modification or combination of the positions for either the dribble, push, or flick, depending upon whether the ball is close or far away, bounding or rolling evenly, or whether the oncoming hit is soft or hard. Though there are three accepted methods of stopping the ball—stick, hand, and foot —the stick is the easiest and quickest to apply. Whatever the method, the player shifts either both feet or her right foot behind the ball to gauge the line as accurately as possible.

STICK STOP

To stop the pace of the ball with the stick, a player slips her right hand down the handle about 6 or 8 inches and holds the stick away from her body to the right, actually in contact with the ground, as she reaches toward the ball. On rough ground, if the ball bumps along, the right hand slips down to the splicing for more control of the stick. If the stick is perpendicular to the ground or even sloping forward (handle away from the body), as stick meets ball, a player can field the ball close to her and not have it running up her stick. Players keep their eyes constantly on the ball and maintain as upright a position as is comfortable.

The stick must be out in front to allow for giving at the moment of contact. Giving with the stick implies a pulling back of the stick with the wrists and arms to lessen the impact and to prevent the ball from bounding away. To stop a hard hit a player may have to move her feet back as well as her stick. Sometimes players relax the grip of both hands just as the ball hits, to relieve the tension and keep the ball close. Players do not relax when fielding a soft pass like the push; instead, they thrust the stick ahead and along the ground to meet the ball as they would in a tackle. They waste no time and either block the ball or push it to a space. When a hard-hit ball approaches, good fielders relax as the impact comes, but employ a quick turn of the wrist almost instantaneously to place the ball to the front or side where they can immediately play it, following a stride backward or forward. Good control of the ball is a matter of eye and wrist.

HAND STOP

Only when players have plenty of time to clear the ball after stopping it is a hand stop advisable. Some fullbacks use it because there is less chance of fumbling the ball and no chance of its bounding far off; some forwards like their center halfback to use it to stop a corner hit for them so that they can immediately step in and drive hard for goal.

Just as in the stick stop, the fielder keeps directly behind the ball. She holds her stick in her left hand out of her way, bends her knees, leans forward, and keeps her right hand in front of her right foot. The ball hits the palm of her hand as she rests her wrist on the ground, and she immediately closes her fingers around the ball to stop it. Time is consumed while the player rises to her feet to place two hands on her stick to drive the ball away.

FOOT STOP

The only reliable way to stop the ball with the foot is to trap it under the instep, the heel maintaining contact with the ground. This stop is the least accurate of the three stops. Players use this only on a smooth field when they are sure the ball will not hit a mound and bounce over.

FIGURE 13. *Stick stop*—Ball at point of contact. Handle of stick is tilted slightly forward to insure a controlled stop. Hands are well apart.

PRACTICE

At the begining of a hockey season, line and backfield players practice all the strokes until they acquire an all-round knowledge of the technique of strokes. It is better to group the more advanced players together in order not to slow up their progress. At times they may be paired off with inexperienced players and instructed to teach and assist the new player. Both will benefit. One reviews her fundamentals; the other witnesses good technique and speeds up in her stroke and field practice. Always set aside separate practices in an endeavor to perfect strokes. Later, forwards and defense members may be separated on the field to concentrate on such techniques as dribbling and centering on the run for wings; passing and shooting at top speed for the inside forwards; dodging, driving, and roll-in practice for halfbacks; clearing and free-hit practice for fullbacks; and stopping forwards' shots for goal and clearing practice for the goalkeeper.

As the ball is hit from a different direction each time, practice running to meet hard drives—stopping them, placing the ball, and clearing. Practice stopping short passes, placing the ball to a partner's advantage. Skillful stickwork eliminates fouling and makes the game of hockey much more interesting.

Chapter III
Line and Backfield Players

To function as a team all eleven players have responsibilities related to the positions they play. Certain positions are handled better by players exhibiting special characteristics. In general, the duties and characteristics are presented here for the five members of the forward line and five of the backfield players, but the goalkeeper's play is discussed in Chapter IX.

FORWARDS

All forwards must be fast runners, quick to start and stop, able to think ahead, pick weaknesses in their opponent's game, and willing to share the honors in team play. To avoid crowding, good forwards space themselves out across the field and keep in their own imaginary playing lanes. They pass on the run, using short passes equally to the right and left sides, and long diagonal passes when an opening occurs in the defense. In the team's own half of the field, forwards play to their wings; in the opponent's half, to the center. Line members receive and carry passes from the left and the right alike without stopping the ball. No forward dribbles *through* an opponent; every forward dribbles in the direction she is *not* going to hit the ball, to throw her opponent off balance. All forwards increase their speed as the play approaches the striking circle and shoot on the run off either foot. A hard drive from the edge of the circle is the best method of attack (Diagrams 7 and 38); nevertheless, when close to the goal a scoop or flick is invaluable (Diagram 37). Too long a backswing on a drive in the scoring area telegraphs the fact that the forward is going to drive and allows the defense member more time to spoil the hit.

To avoid being marked closely and to help the defense select openings, forwards constantly move around to create spaces for passes and always run to meet a pass. Since defense players often are leisurely dribblers, forwards tackle back as soon as they have lost the ball to the opposing team, allowing their own backfield time to mark and cover. In doing this, though, they must be careful not to run back on their own backfield members. When the ball is driven toward an oncoming opponent, forwards rush their opponent rather than hold back with the idea that they may intercept the opponent's hit. No line player enters the striking circle when her own backfield is defending the goal; she awaits to move to a pass near the 25-yard line. To field a ball advantageously on a corner hit and to bully well are essential to good forward play. Capable line members combine foot- and stickwork with headwork, cooperate with one another under all circumstances, and never forget that they are obligated to the team to *attack*.

CENTER FORWARD

Center forward, the pivot of the team, the most closely marked forward, excels in stickwork. If she is master of the bully, her team has a psychological as well as a material advantage on the first play. She dribbles the ball close to her, conceals the direction of her passes, divides the play equally to either side, and opens up the game with long drives to her wings. She goes toward passes to nip in before the opposing center halfback and drops back toward the circle to help in defending, if her opposing center halfback backs up her own line players closely and is good at shooting. The center forward rarely tackles back; however, when the opposing center halfback has the ball, center forward does not permit her to dribble unimpeded. She always keeps her central position in the field; therefore, she is the player who warns her teammates when they are out of position or offside.

INNERS

The first duty of the inners is to feed the wings; the second, to tackle back energetically—more than any one of the other three forwards. Like the center forward, inners dribble the ball under perfect control, close to the stick, and field the ball on a corner hit in the same manner. Inners converge toward the center forward in two instances: first, when the center is bullying; second, when they themselves are approaching the striking circle. In the circle, both inners rush almost everyone's shots for goal (Diagram 7). A wing approaching the striking area passes to her near inner or center forward; far inner is always alert in case the others fumble. Inners must be clever in their use of the scoop, the flick, the push, and the right and left drives if they are to be of value in attack. They are familiar with the use of the back, square, and diagonal pass in the striking circle (Diagram 4).

Right Inner. Some persons assume the right-inner position to be the easier inner position to play because the drive to the left, a comparatively simple stroke, is her main standby. To counteract this assumption, it is pointed out that the right inner, unless she passes to her own right wing or dodges, is forced to pass to the stick side of her opponent. Also, when she anticipates a centering pass from her wing, right inner has to move her feet into a position to receive the ball from the right and field it closely to prevent her opposing left fullback from intercepting. Perfect timing, accurate placements, and close fielding, then, are required.

Left Inner. The difficulties in the left-inner position lie with the receiving of passes in the circle, the shooting for goal, and the dribbling. In the first instance, left inner, with her left shoulder toward the goal, twists her body to receive the ball behind her; in the second place, left inner makes a half-turn with her shoulders while on the run, if she is to shoot for goal with any degree of accuracy; in the third place, left inner is slightly ahead of or on line with the ball when she dribbles and keeps the ball on her right instead of in front of her. Because left wing has difficulty picking up passes coming to her from the left, left inner does not drive too hard or too far forward to her left. A pass to the nonstick side of her opposing right fullback sets up openings for the center forward, if the left inner remembers to direct a diagonal pass *behind* the opposing center halfback when she is marking the center forward closely, or a square pass when the center halfback is marking loosely.

Left inner rushes every shot for goal and tackles back more than any line member. It is she who is the most aggressive forward and who needs to possess the most endurance.

WINGS

To save balls from going over the side lines, wings play out near the side, keep ahead of their line on the opponents' half of the field, and keep even with the forwards on their half of the field. They are the best dribblers, realizing that they dribble loosely when the alley is free and they have evaded their opposing halfback, to keep her from recovering. Used properly their most effective dodge is the scoop.

At the 25-yard line wings flick or drive to center on an angle, so that the ball can be fielded on the run by their inners. Those who err in carrying the ball too close to the end line allow the opposing defense time to mark the other attacking forwards closely and reduce to a minimum the openings for other forwards to score. When a teammate takes a roll-in, wings dash up the alley in an attempt to shake off their opposing halfback; when an opponent rolls the ball in, wings are alert to intercept a reverse roll. Wings take the roll-in near the scoring area (Diagrams 9 and 10), and all corner hits (Diagrams 25 and 27). Tackling back occurs in but one situation—when the wings' own halfbacks are too far down the field.

Right Wing. Right wing centers the ball more easily if it is ahead of her; so she uses the loose dribble. To prevent the ball from going out of bounds, she may employ the left-hand lunge for added reach. Right wing awaits a pass near the 5-yard line to receive it on her right but dribbles the ball near the side line to make it more difficult for her opposing halfback to tackle. It is imperative that right wing play in the alley, but she sometimes should cut in on her opposing halfback if she is in a position to intercept an oncoming ball.

Left Wing. Left wing may use a "stroking" dribble, with the ball almost behind her right foot in order to be in a position to pass the ball in quickly with the right drive or flick. She awaits a pass practically in an out-of-bounds position to draw her opposing halfback to the alley. Left wing finds the reversed-stick dodge a good one to employ and knows how to pull the ball back with a reversed stick if she gets too close to the goal line before she can center the ball.

BACKFIELD PLAYERS

All defense players must possess endurance and confidence, make decisions quickly, run fast, cooperate with line and backfield players, and understand thoroughly one another's team play. They not only back up their forwards in an attack, tackle quickly, field the ball accurately, glance up to pick spaces before passing, and anticipate and intercept passes but also defend their goal through a system of marking and covering (see pages 81-84). They can seldom rest. If they are not well behind their forwards in attack, it is essential that they race back to defend. All know how to clear the ball with a hard, clean hit (Diagram 6) but never use the long hit if a short pass will suffice.

CENTER HALFBACK

The hardest-worked player on the team is the center halfback. She must not only mark the forward who is in the best position to shoot for goal, but also back up her own forward line constantly. She never wanders, neither does she cover. Upon her rests the responsibility for dividing the play to each side of the field and for directing the maneuvers of her own defense members.

Defensively, center halfback's main assignment is to bottle up her opposing center forward—to intercept passes to her and to prevent her from shooting. She leaves her opponent *only* if several of her own defense are left behind and it remains for her to stop the attack; and, in the circle, she must sometimes leave her center forward to rush out to tackle her opposing center halfback, if the latter carries the ball toward the circle with intent to shoot for goal. She stays on the stick of her opposing forward in the circle in order not to block the goalkeeper's view. When spaces to her forwards are blocked, she clears to her wing halfback or fullback to open out the game. Within the area of the two 25-yard lines, center halfback marks her opponent loosely, for opponents' passes, generally, are directed to the wings, and she intends to intercept rather than to mark closely. At a center bully she waits to the left of those bullying, to protect herself on her nonstick side (Diagram 28). She is alert to determine which one of her opponents' fullbacks is covering, in order that her first pass can be to the free inner.

Offensively, center halfback steadies the ball before hitting it; and, since hers is a congested area of the field, she sizes up situations and knows when to pass directly to her forwards, when to pass through to space, or when to draw out her opposing center halfback. In the latter instance, if her own center forward is free, center halfback never dribbles up to draw out the opponent. She always backs up her center forward; near the striking area, she assists in backing up the inners because her fullbacks never come to the edge of the circle. When she takes a free hit near the circle (Diagram 21), rather than the customary short pass to a space near one of the three inside forwards, center halfback may catch her opponents off guard by directing her hit to an unmarked wing.

Many times center halfback is unmarked on the edge of the striking circle; more often, when her own line is near the mouth of the goal, the opponents clear the ball in her direction. Whenever it is possible, center halfback shoots for goal; her own center forward rushes the shot.

Because center halfback backs up her line closely, her most difficult assignment is to overtake her opposing center forward when the ball shifts to the possession of her opponents (Diagrams 32, 34, and 35).

WING HALFBACKS

Defensively, a wing halfback either marks her opposing wing when the ball is within her territory or covers. If the play is in the middle of the field, wing halfbacks mark loosely to be in a position to intercept passes to the wings. When her own fullback covers in a central position, wing halfback covers opposite the inner position and exchanges duties with the fullback if the situation arises. Wing halfbacks and fullbacks work in close association; however, in their eagerness to assist, halfbacks must not trespass in fullback territory (see page 83). They are alert in the striking area for hard clears from the goaler or fullbacks which they relay to their own wings.

Offensively, a wing halfback feeds her wing with a hard drive ahead to permit the wing to pick up the ball on a run, with a dodge and a pass, or with a scoop, if the opposing halfback is blocking the spaces to the wing. To vary her play, the wing halfback passes to an unmarked inner; the inner has a wider angle in which to relay the pass to the wing. Halfbacks take many of the roll-ins (Diagrams 11-16) and free hits (Diagrams 18-20) and back up the line members when the ball is on their side of the field.

Wing halfbacks are untiring players, responsible for tackling, backing up, marking, and covering to a greater extent than the other backfield members (Diagrams 30-36).

Right Halfback. A thorough knowledge of the right drive and the left-hand lunge are essential to the repertory of the right halfback. She employs the drive for feeding her wing and inner, and the left-hand lunge for tackling back. In the use of the latter stroke, right halfback must be careful not to hit the ball over the side line. To keep on the stick side of her opposing wing, she plays near the 5-yard line; to cover, she drops back slightly deeper than does her own left halfback. If her opposing left wing plays the ball close to the goal line, right halfback is on the watch for the wing's stratagem of reversing her stick to pull the ball back and dodge. Right halfback performs the roll-in with her left hand to allow a maximum freedom of swing.

Left Halfback. Of the two halfback positions, left is the more arduous. She opposes the easier wing position; she is drawn out in the alley to mark her opponent on the stick side; she does much of her tackling back on the non-stick side of her opponent, necessitating an adept usage of the circular tackle, right-hand lunge, and right cut. To pick up a diagonal pass from an opposing line player, she circles around the ball in order not to send it out of bounds. Unless left halfback fields the ball on her stick side, she resorts to the reverse-stick stroke and is likely to obstruct. Left halfback executes the roll-in with her right hand.

Fullbacks

Fullbacks, working as a pair, always maintain an oblique position: one covers, ready to block up holes in the defense or intercept long through-passes; the other backs up her own line or marks her opponent. Whenever the ball is passed from one side of the field to the other, the fullbacks shift their positions automatically. No matter how close their forwards are to scoring a goal, one fullback remains near the center line. The fullback who covers deep drifts toward the center of the field (see page 83).

Defensively, fullbacks dodge rather than dribble to send the ball toward the wings; clear the ball with long hits to the wings or, when the ball is near the goal cage, to the halfbacks; and field hard oncoming drives before passing them. When the ball is close to the goal and the fullback is in the goaler's way, she steps aside to permit the goalkeeper to play the ball. One fullback is up near the center halfback at the time of a center bully. As a rule, this player is the right fullback (Diagram 28); she marks loosely on the stick side of her opposing left inner, because the majority of the opponents' first passes are directed to their left (opponents are hurried and use the drive to the left). Each fullback backs up inner bullies on her side of the field (Diagram 29). When the attack fouls in the striking circle, fullbacks take the free hit (Diagram 24.) Fullbacks mark inners closely in the scoring area.

Left fullback overtakes her opponent on the nonstick side, uses the circular tackle, and is ready to replace center halfback when she is left behind (see page 84). It is the left back who covers deep when the ball is in the center as well as on her right side of the field. In the striking circle, rather than marking on the stick side of the inner in the manner of the right fullback, left back prevents her opponent from having a clear path to goal by marking directly in front of her.

Offensively, fullbacks, if they are fast runners, back up their own forwards at least as far as their opponents' 25-yard line, when the ball is on their side of the field. There are coaches, though, who prefer that both backs go no farther than the center line.

Goalkeeper

A goalkeeper possesses courage, confidence, and common sense. Her mind as well as her body is agile; she keeps her eye constantly on the ball. She knows her own team's setup for defense, often warns her players of unmarked forwards in the striking circle, and calls to her defense if she intends to tackle so that the backfield player can take the goaler's place in the cage. Above all, the goaler must study the technique of her opponents in an effort to determine their manner of playing the ball in the circle and make instantaneous decisions when the occasions arise.

For discussion of goalkeeping duties, see page 85 and Chapter IX, Goaltending.

Chapter IV
Passing, Clearing, Shooting, and Dodging

Before any hockey player is instructed how to mark, cover, or back up, she should understand thoroughly how to pass, clear, shoot, and dodge. Many of these tactics are learned along with instruction in the technique of the strokes, or with a knowledge of the individual player's responsibilities. A detailed review of the tactics, however, is not out of place; and, before the players learn about their relation to the team and opponents, they should be thoroughly familiar with the several means of playing the ball.

Actually, clearing is considered a defense player's duty—passing the ball away from the mouth of the goal; shooting is explained as an offensive player's duty—passing the ball directly at the mouth of the goal; dodging, passing to oneself, is a duty of any player. Accurate passes depend on the judgment and skill of the individual player. Merely hitting the ball is not passing.

PASSING

Psychological moments for passes occur when the player is about to be tackled, when the opponent is out of position, or when there is an opening on the field. Each pass should be accurately timed. Good passers never give away the direction the ball is to be sent; they aim before passing, carefully surveying the positions of the opponents in order to place their hits to the exact spot intended. Everyone runs toward any pass that is traveling slowly; otherwise it will be intercepted by an opponent. The passer rarely follows the pass—the receiver knows she is expected to get it.

BACKFIELD TO FORWARD LINE

A forward finds it difficult to pick up a ball that is coming to her from behind, when the ball is not sent to her in a good position for handling. Careless backfield players make some passes too long and others too short, or direct their passes to the nonstick side of the receiver. In these cases, forwards have to slow up considerably to run back for the ball or to circle around to pick it up. Responsible defense players realize that the attack begins when they obtain possession of the ball and take time to accurately direct the passes squarely or diagonally forward.

Dependable receivers hold themselves in the most advantageous position for receiving the ball, that is, with toes pointing in the direction of their goal, bodies turned to the right so that they are looking back for the ball over their right shoulders, left shoulders leading toward the goal, and sticks down. To receive on the right, left wing stands near the side line and the other forwards anywhere in their approximate "lanes" in the field. To receive on the left, players sometimes await the ball with their right shoulder leading, looking back over their left.

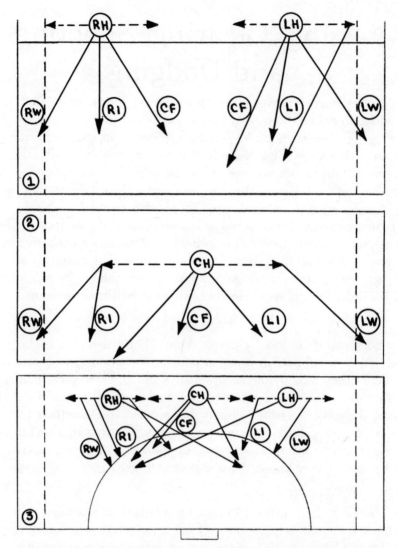

Diagram 2. *Passing: backfield to forward line.* (1) Wing halfbacks. (2) Center halfback. (3) Halfbacks to forward line near the circle.

Diagram 2 illustrates to whom the left halfback, center halfback, and right halfback pass and to what side of the forward the pass is directed. In general, halfbacks or fullbacks feed forwards on the right (stick) side, and fullbacks feed halfbacks on the right. Left halfback is the one backfield member who may not be able to feed left inner or center forward on the right side. If left halfback is out in the alley, her pass to the left inner or center forward has to be a long, diagonal one up the left side and well ahead of these forwards.

When the forwards reach the 25-yard line, all backfield drives are directed toward the center. As the circle is aproached a few players may be fed well ahead on their left side, that is, right wing from right halfback, right inner from center halfback.

Circle Play

When left wing takes a corner or penalty corner, she drives the ball to a teammate's stick at the edge of the circle. The player stops it and immediately drives for goal. Diagram 3 illustrates both the left wing and right wing play at corner and penalty corner hits.

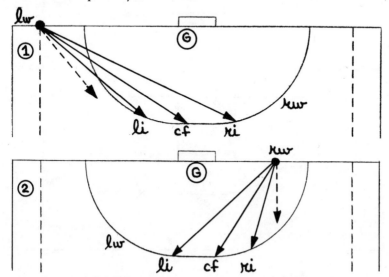

DIAGRAM 3. *Passing: circle play.* (1) Left wing to line players on a corner. (2) Right wing to line players on a penalty corner.

Forward-line play

Against coordinated defense players who are marking, only direct, quick, deceptive passes are successful. Described below and illustrated in Diagram 4 are passes for line players to try in the striking circle area. Executed well, they should help forwards penetrate a defense.

1. Back pass from either inner to her center forward. Center forward drives for either corner of the goal without first stopping the ball. (To avoid being called for offside, the inner, after the pass, may have to run over the goal line and remain out of bounds until the result of the play is determined.) If necessary, left inner uses a reversed stick for this pass; right inner uses the natural drive. Sometimes a reversed-stick stroke is the only stroke a player has time to use to keep the ball from going over the goal line.

2. Square pass across the circle by either wing. The wing may use this pass from a roll-in or free-hit position, or may use it just outside the circle following a dribble to the edge. Any one of the forward-line members drives for goal without first stopping the ball. Forwards can use the square pass near the goal area whenever their opponents are marking loosely.

3. Drive from left wing, on a corner or penalty corner, to center forward. Center forward stops the ball, then makes a square pass to left inner who shoots for either corner of the goal. This drive may go to the right inner who makes a square pass to center forward who shoots.

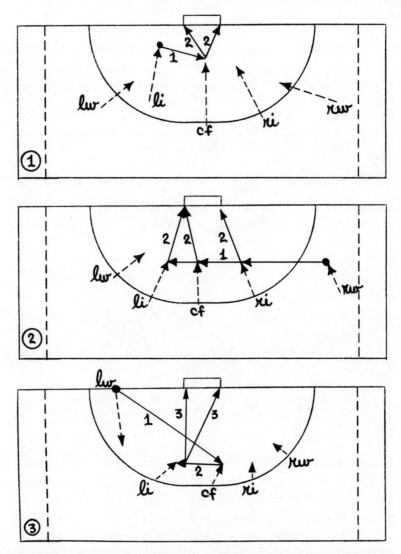

DIAGRAM 4. *Passing in the striking circle.* (1) Backpass from left inner to center forward [1] who shoots [2]. (2) Square pass from right wing to line players [1] who shoot [2]. (3) From penalty corner position, diagonal pass from left wing to center forward [1], square pass from center forward to lift inner [2] who shoots [3].

Players must know how to control a variety of passes, distribute them to the right and left, drive them hard and long, or push, flick, or scoop them. To succeed in breaking through a defense the player must be deceptive. Diagram 5 shows several kinds of passes, which are described below, that players can use anywhere in the field of play.

1. Diagonal pass from any one player to a neighbor. This pass is disconcerting to the opposing defense if the forward passes to the teammate on her right (nonstick side of the defense player who has started to tackle), and the teammate immediately returns the pass. This is called a triangular pass. Sometimes

two opponents are left behind, if the combination of the pass to the right and the return pass is performed well (Diagram 35).

2. Combination of square pass and diagonal pass. This works well when an inner who is behind her own forward-line players (because of tackling back or marking on a free hit or a roll-in) cannot get back on line with her center forward or wing who has the ball. A square pass is made to the inner who returns the ball by a diagonal pass ahead to a teammate. The combination pass also works well with a square pass from either fullback to her own wing halfback who makes a long diagonal pass to inner or wing.

3. Long diagonal pass across the field from a wing to her own far inner. Though left wing uses this pass, right wing is in the better position because she can drive to the left more easily than left wing can drive to the right. A long diagonal pass upsets the opposing defense since the covering defenders are immediately called upon to break up the play. Whenever players use a long, through pass they never drive it quite so hard to the left side of the field as to the right side, because the players on the left have more difficulty fielding the ball than do those on the right.

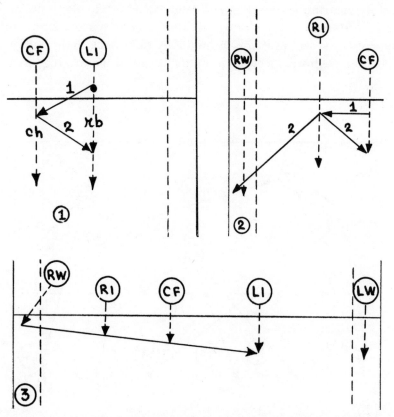

DIAGRAM 5. *Useful passes in the field of play.* (1) Triangular pass from left inner to center forward [1] who returns the ball to left inner [2]. (2) Combination of square pass [1] and diagonal pass [2] from center forward to right inner who sends the ball to either center forward or right wing. (3) Long diagonal pass across the field from right wing to left inner.

CLEARING

It is most important that all defense players know that they do not clear the ball across the striking circle and rarely clear down the center of the field. In the circle, right halfback and right fullback clear the ball to the right (right drive), left fullback and left halfback clear to the left (left drive, the easier of the two drives). Goalkeeper and center halfback may clear to either side.

In the territory ranging from outside the circle to the far 25-yard line, the five defense players clear in several ways: right back to right halfback, to right wing, or to the opposite side of the field; right halfback to right wing or to the opposite side of the field; center halfback to either side of the field; left back to left halfback or to left wing; and left halfback to left wing. Therefore, between the two 25-yard lines, the best clears are directed out toward the sides of the field (center halfback may sometimes pass to her own center forward) to draw the opposing backfield players toward the alleys.

It is not advised that left back and left halfback change the direction of the ball by clearing across the field, because it is difficult to make a right drive go that far. In midfield, however, left back may clear across the field. The longest clears will probably be made by right back, right half, or center half. Diagram 6 illustrates clears in midfield and in the striking circle.

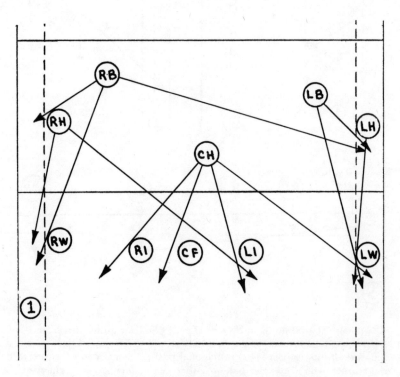

DIAGRAM 6. *Clearing.* (1) Players in midfield.

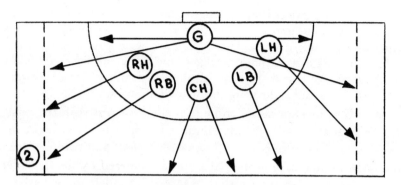

DIAGRAM 6 *(Continued)*. (2) Defense players in the striking circle.

SHOOTING

Line players should learn to drive a ball as hard as any backfield member, for they use the drive almost every time they reach the circle. They increase their speed just before this shot and shoot on the run off either foot. Because they take aim while dribbling, there is no pause in the circle. The corners of the goal afford the best place to aim, especially the corner on the nonstick side of the goalkeeper. All players who shoot for goal keep their left shoulders toward the direction of the intended shot. The backward lift of the stroke is short to avoid wasting time, and added force comes from snapping the wrists just before the ball is hit. When a forward drives for goal she rushes her own shot (or the goal) with her stick down, and the other members of the forward line must know immediately who is responsible for rushing the goal to support the driver.

Diagram 7 shows the actions of teammates as each member of the forward line shoots for goal. A description of each of the five situations follows:

1. Left inner drives from the edge of the circle and follows to the goal. Right inner rushes the goal to support left inner. Both right and left sides of the goal are covered, and a goalkeeper's attempt to clear to the right or left may result in the ball's being picked up by either inner. Center forward may either rush the goal or stay back to see whether the ball is cleared down the center of the circle or back of either of the two inners who are rushing. In any case, the center forward is in a good position to try to score. Wings stay out near the edge of the circle to take any clear that is too far out to the side for inside forwards to handle.

2. Center forward drives from the edge of the circle and follows to the goal. Left inner rushes the goal to support center forward on her nonstick side. Right inner may rush the goal but both wings remain back to watch the direction of the goalkeeper's or a back's clears and to try intercepting them.

3. Right inner drives from the edge of the circle and follows her own shot. Left inner rushes the goal to support right inner on her nonstick side. Center forward may rush but wings remain back to intercept clears.

4. Right wing drives from the edge of the circle and right inner rushes the shot. Left inner rushes the goal to support right inner on the nonstick side. Center forward may rush. Right wing and left wing stay back for clears.

5. Left wing drives from the edge of the circle and left inner follows the shot. Right inner rushes the goal to support left inner. Center forward may rush. Left wing and right wing stay back for clears.

The drawings in Diagram 7 show that the forwards rush the goal in an inverted W formation which has originated from a fairly straight line formation. A driver and a supporter always rush a shot, and two or three members stay back to take care of the balls that are cleared by the defenders just beyond the players rushing the shot. Observe that left inner rushes every drive for goal; left inner is on the nonstick side of every line player except left wing. Center forward has an alternative: she may rush the goal or hold back to watch for clears on every drive for goal. Right inner rushes left-inner and right-and left-wing drives. Wings generally remain out near the edge of the circle. If a wing is drawn in the circle and is in a position to try for

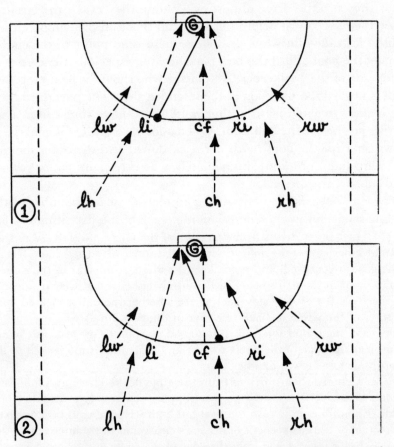

DIAGRAM 7. *Shooting and rushing the ball and goal.* (1) Left inner shoots and rushes the goal; right inner supports; center forward may rush or hold back. (2) Center forward shoots and rushes the goal, left inner supports.

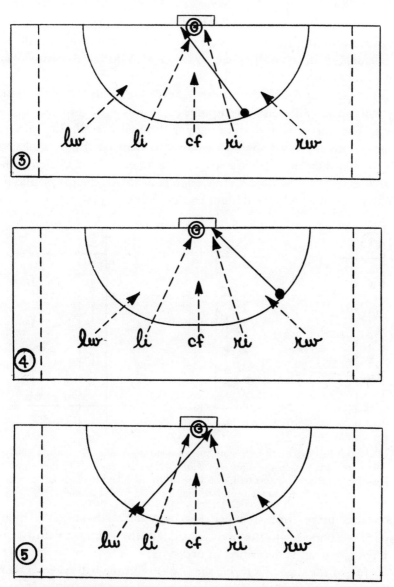

DIAGRAM 7 *(Continued)*. (3) Right inner shoots and rushes the goal; left inner supports; center forward may rush or hold back. (4) Right wing shoots; left inner and right inner rush the goal; center forward may rush or hold back. (5) Left wing shoots; left inner and right inner rush the goal; center forward may rush or hold back.

goal, she rushes her own shot, while the nearer inner switches positions and assumes the wing's duties near the edge of the circle.

If center halfback or wing halfbacks have possession of the ball at the edge of the circle, they shoot for goal rather than pass to a line player. In these instances the halfbacks do not follow the shot; all three inside forwards rush it.

DODGING

Accurate dodging involves speed in execution, timing, and deception, and is performed in a small space. A successful dodge depends upon the element of surprise.

Both forwards and defense players employ dodging as an alternative to passing when a player must rely upon herself alone to get the ball past an opponent. The player who dodges regains the ball herself. She may pass to a teammate to avoid losing the ball as her opponent tackles back or continue on with the ball herself. Dodging will not disconcert the opponents, though, as much as short passes, because a dodge is a slower means of playing the ball. When a defense player dodges in the vicinity of the circle, she allows

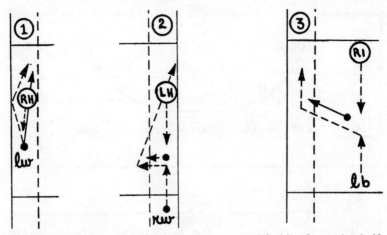

DIAGRAM 8. *Dodges.* (1) Left wing passes to nonstick side of opposing half-back, regains ball in the alley. (2) Right wing pulls the ball to the left as opponent tackles, regains ball, and keeps it in the alley. (3) Left back uses a left-hand lunge on a free ball, keeps it from opponent.

the opponents more time to mark her own forwards closely. Diagram 8 illustrates three dodges—to the nonstick side, to the left, and with a left-hand lunge. Each situation is described in order.

1. Just at the time of a tackle the player with the ball makes a short pass to the nonstick (right) side of her opponent and runs around the opponent on the left to pick up the ball again.

2. Just at the time of a tackle the dribbler pulls or taps the ball across her body to the left, as she swerves to the left, and then regains the ball and continues on down the side of the field. The ball-carrier may use a reverse stroke to pull or tap the ball to her right—the pull across is just enough to throw the tackler off balance.

3. As two opponents approach the ball, one reaches out with a left-hand lunge and taps the ball to the left just as her opponent starts to hit the ball. The lunger swerves to the left, picks up the ball, and prepares to pass. This is a difficult maneuver, used by experienced players only. It is much better if the first player who reaches the ball controls it and uses 1 or 2 described above.

Chapter V
The Roll-In

During a game when the ball goes out of bounds over either side line, it is put back into play from the point where it crossed the side line by a member of the team opposite to the player who last touched the ball. The player who returns the ball in play does so by hand. This hand technique is called the roll-in.

The roller must hit the ground with the ball within 1 yard of the point where it left the field (this yard measured along the line travelled by the ball), must not spin or bounce the ball in rolling it, and must have her feet and stick outside the side line at the time of the roll. A team whose players are adept in the technique of the roll gains an immediate advantage, since these players will take the roll-in quickly before the opponents have an opportunity to get set and mark possible receivers and will vary their tactics to keep the opponents guessing as to whom the roll will be directed.

To roll the ball into the field of play, a player grasps it in her fingers and swings her arm back from the shoulder and then vigorously forward as she steps forward with the opposite foot, knee bent deeply. Players on the right side of the field roll the ball with their left hand; those on the left, with their right hand. This affords a free arm and shoulder action. As the player releases the ball the trunk is bent forward, the hand is close to the ground (to prevent the ball from lofting or bouncing), and the weight has shifted to the forward foot. The force and distance of the roll generally depends upon the amount of backswing of the arm. On a roll directed to the side or back (reverse-roll) rather than ahead, the roller checks her arm when it is perpendicular to the ground and changes the direction of the swing before the release of the ball. See Figure 14, below, and Figure 15, page 58.

FIGURE 14. *Roll-in*—(A) Start of roll-in: shows arm well back and body close to the ground. This player is on the left side of the field; hence she rolls with her right hand. (B) Point of release: shows position of the hand with the ball and the weight on the forward foot.

Generally, wing halfbacks are the ones who take a roll-in; therefore, the majority of the illustrations on roll-ins which appear later on in this chapter are concerned with the halfbacks and the variety of plays they may use.

All players should know that halfbacks send the ball down the field to their inners or wings, or roll sometimes to center halfback (especially when the opposing center halfback has left this player unmarked), or in rare instances *reverse-roll* to their fullbacks (a surprise tactic); and that inners mark the opposing inner. Since the attacking inner generally goes out to the 5-yard line to be in a better position to receive the ball should the pass come to her, the opposing inner follows her and marks her closely.

When a wing takes the roll-in near her opponent's goal line, her inner does not go out as far as the 5-yard line. Either the opposing inner or fullback marks the offensive inner, depending upon how near the circle the inner is playing. Wings usually roll directly across to the striking area to a space ahead of an inner or center forward and behind the opposing defense; sometimes, however, they roll to their halfback who may be in a better position to pick up the ball.

Fullbacks take a roll-in only when the ball goes out of bounds near the center of the field and the fullback's own teammates are far up the field. In this situation quick action on the part of the attacking fullback may mean that the opponents will not have time to mark the attackers. Thus a fullback roll-in to her own halfback or down the field to her own inner may catch the opponents off guard.

The person who receives a roll-in should immediately pass to someone else, unless, in the case of a wing, she can continue down the alley with the ball. If center halfback or fullback receives the roll-in, a hard drive to the opposite side of the field is disconcerting to the opponents and opens up the play.

ROLL-IN SITUATIONS

Diagrams 9-13 illustrate situations resulting from the fact that the ball has been hit out of bounds over the side lines. The player taking the roll is a member of the team which did not cause the ball to go out of bounds. This player cannot roll if anyone stands within the 5-yard line or outside the side line. Players on both teams, then, must be alert to keep in the field of play and remain 5 yards from the roller. (If, in the umpire's opinion, a defender stands within the 5-yard line to delay the roll-in, she should not stop the game.) The diagrams show the places where defensive and offensive players should be to block the play (defensive) or to execute one successfully (offensive). Needless to mention that all players will *not* be in these "perfect" places. If everyone could mark, back up, or cover exactly as illustrated there might be no incentive for a contest.

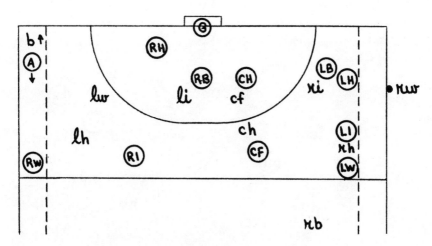

DIAGRAM 9. *Wing roll-in near the goal line.*

DIAGRAM 9. Team A hits the ball out of bounds near the goal line. Team *b wing* takes the roll-in, in order not to draw her own wing halfback too far up the field. (Illustrated by *rw* taking the roll.)

DEFENSIVE TEAM—A

LB, RB, and CH mark *ri, li,* and *cf.*
LH plays out toward the alley, ready to pick up *rw* after the roll.
RH covers.
CF drops back to mark *ch* loosely, unless *ch* is well into the circle.
LI marks *rh* who goes out to the 5-yard line. LI will be drawn out of her forward line.
LW, RI, and RW keep out near the 25-yard line. RI and RW anticipate a long diagonal pass if LI or CF get the ball, that is, if either player intercepts a roll-in pass from *rw* to her *rh* or her *ch*. LW stands at the 5-yard line, ready for a pass if her LI gets the ball.

OFFENSIVE TEAM—*b*

rw may roll to *ri, rh,* or to some space in the circle in the hope that one of her line players can get by the opponent who is marking.
ri does not go out to the 5-yard line. She may wish to run toward a pass from her *rw*.
All halfbacks back up the forward line. *rh* and *ch* will be marked closely by their opponents.
rb watches LW since the play is on her side of the field.
lb covers (not shown).

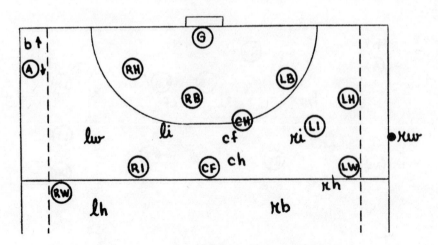

DIAGRAM 10. *Wing roll-in on the goal side of the 25-yard line.*

DIAGRAM 10. Team A hits the ball out of bounds on the goal side of the 25-yard line, Team *b wing* takes the roll-in. (Illustrated by *rw* taking the roll.)

DEFENSIVE TEAM—A

> LI marks *ri,* since *ri* is not close to the striking circle.
> LH plays back, ready to pick up *rw* after the roll.
> LB and RB are alert for inners as they come into the circle.
> CH marks *cf.*
> LW marks *rh.*
> RH covers.
> CF watches *ch.* RI and RW play out near the 25-yard line in anticipation of a long diagonal pass if a teammate gets the ball.
>
> *Note:* If *ri* plays ahead of *rw* (she must be careful that she is not offside) and if *ri* is near the circle, LB will mark the inner. The situation, then, will be practically the same as the one illustrated in Diagram 9.

OFFENSIVE TEAM—b

> *rw* may roll to *ri, cf,* or *rh*—to any one of the three who is not marked by an opponent. She may roll the ball to a space ahead of her own line.
> *ri* does not go out to the 5-yard line. She remains in a position so that she can run to meet a roll.
> *ch* and *rh* back up their line players.
> *lh* covers. She must be in a position to watch RW and RI in case of a shift of play to her side of the field.
> *rb* plays up since the action is on her side of the field.
> *lb* covers near center line (not shown).

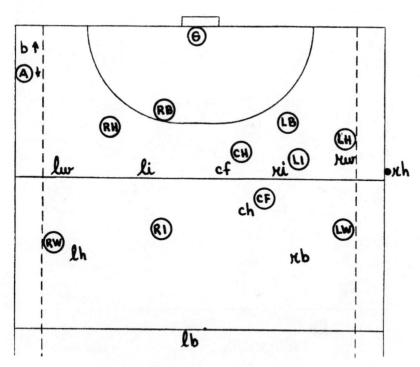

DIAGRAM 11. *Halfback roll-in at the 25-yard line.*

DIAGRAM 11. Team A hits the ball out of bounds at the 25-yard line. Team *b halfback* takes the roll -in. (Illustrated by *rh* taking the roll.)

DEFENSIVE TEAM—A

LI (drawn out of her forward line), CH, and LH mark *ri, cf,* and *rw.* CF keeps on the stick side of *ch.*

LB is ready to mark or tackle if the ball remains with the offense, or back up if her own team secures the ball. RB and RH cover.

RI keeps on line with LW.

RW is farther up the field, expecting a long diagonal pass if a member of her team intercepts the ball.

OFFENSIVE TEAM—b

rh may roll to *ri, rw,* or *ch*—any one of the three who is not marked.

ri does not go out as far as the 5-yard line and keeps shifting her position to avoid being marked by her opponent. All forwards keep on line with one another.

ch keeps alert for a possible pass from *rh.*

rb backs up her players on her side of the field. *lh* and *lb* cover.

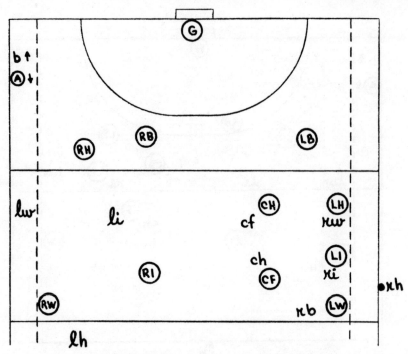

DIAGRAM 12. *Halfback roll-in between 25-yard and center lines.*

DIAGRAM 12. Team A hits the ball out of bounds between the 25-yard and center lines. Team *b halfback* takes the roll-in. (Illustrated by *rh* rolling.)

DEFENSIVE TEAM—A

LH marks *rw;* LI marks *ri* in order not to draw LB far out of position.
CF marks *ch* and keeps between her and *rh.*
CH marks *cf.* LB, RB, and RH cover.
LW and RW play ahead of the other forwards in their line, hoping for an intercepted ball by a teammate and a long forward drive to either side of the field. RI keeps on line with her own CF.

OFFENSIVE TEAM—*b*

rh may roll to *rw, ri, cf* (Diagram 15), or *ch* (Diagram 14).
rw plays up the field, near the 5-yard line.
ri is close to the 5-yard line, either opposite *rh* or between *rh* and *rw.*
cf, li, lw are on line with *rw.*
ch backs up the forward line and keeps alert for a possible pass from *rh.*
rb backs up her own team; *lh* covers.
lb covers in the center of the field near the 25-year line (not shown).

Note: On the other side of the field *lh* may roll to *li* or to *lw* (Diagram 16). On either side, fullback may take the roll-in to save time, if the other members of her team are far up the field. Not advised, however.

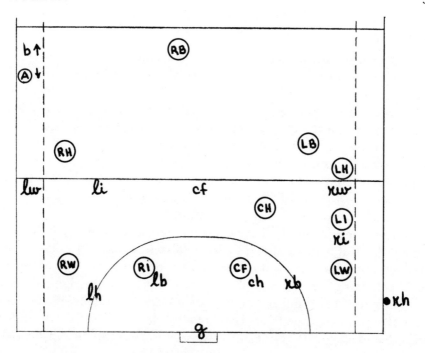

DIAGRAM 13. *Halfback roll-in near own goal line.*

DIAGRAM 13. Team A hits the ball out of bounds close to the opponents' goal line. Team *b halfback* takes the roll-in. (Illustrated by *rh* taking the roll.)

DEFENSIVE TEAM—A

> LI marks *ri* who leaves her forward line to play closer to *rh*. LI is ready to intercept the roll-in if it comes down the alley.
> Other line players play ahead of LI—in the scoring area.
> LW tries to play between *rh* and *rb*.
> LH marks *rw*.
> LB backs up her teammates; CH backs up her own forward line.
> RH and RB cover.

OFFENSIVE TEAM—*b*

> *rh* may pass hard up the alley to *ri* or to *rw*. The distance to *rw* may be too far; *ri* should be ready to relay the pass to *rw*.
> *cf, li,* and *lw* keep on line with *rw*.
> *ch* marks CF and watches CH. *lb* marks RI.
> *rb* watches LW, marks her if she comes into the striking circle.
> *lh* covers.

Note: *lh* will find conditions similar if she rolls on her side of the field. *lw* should be prepared to cross over the alley, even to run outside the side line, so she can pick up the pass on her stick side.

ROLL-IN PLAYS

The halfback, who generally takes the roll-in anywhere between the two 25-yard lines, uses any one of a number of passes. Members of her forward line as well as the backfield players should practice several different roll-in plays with both right and left halfbacks. A team with a variety of plays which are executed quickly keeps an opposing team on the move and guessing.

The success of a roll-in play depends largely upon how well a team marks its opponents and how quickly a roller can take the roll before every player is marked. No one should look the way she intends to roll the ball. Anyone taking a roll-in should follow her pass immediately. Diagram 14 shows a right halfback rolling to her center halfback. This is a surprise play and should be attempted only if the center halfback is not marked. This play is more difficult if it is attempted by left halfback on the other side of the field, because center halfback will not be in a position to drive to right inner without first fielding the ball and placing it for a drive to the right. Fielding the ball consumes time, but if center halfback is especially adept in her stick-work the play might be tried. Usually a roll-in from the the left halfback to center halfback would result in a pass back to the same side of the field—to left inner or left wing.

FIGURE 15. *Start of roll-in.* This player is on the right side of the field; hence she rolls with her left hand.

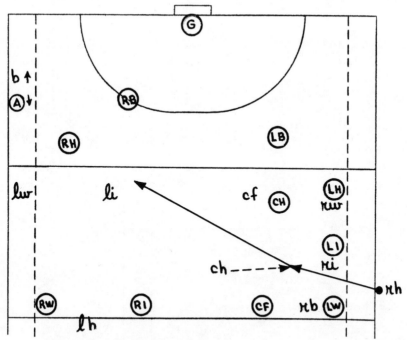

DIAGRAM 14. *Roll-in play: right halfback to her center halfback.*

DIAGRAM 14. Team A hits the ball out of bounds in midfield. Team *b half-back* takes the roll-in. If *ri* is not playing opposite *rh* and if *ch* is not marked, this play may be pulled as a surprise. (Illustrated by *rh* rolling to *ch*.)

DEFENSIVE TEAM—A

LH marks *rw*.
LI marks *ri*.
CF does not drop out of her line to mark *ch*—the reason this play is possible.
LB, RB, and RH cover.
LW, CF, RI, and RW play on line with one another.

OFFENSIVE TEAM—b

rh rolls toward *ch* who runs to meet the ball and immediately directs it across the field and ahead to *li*.
rw is up the field and close to the 5-yard line.
ri is close to the 5-yard line but is not directly opposite *rh*.
cf, li, lw are on line with *rw*.
rb backs up her own teammates, since the action is on her side of the field.
lh covers.
lb covers in the center of the field near the 25-yard line (not shown).

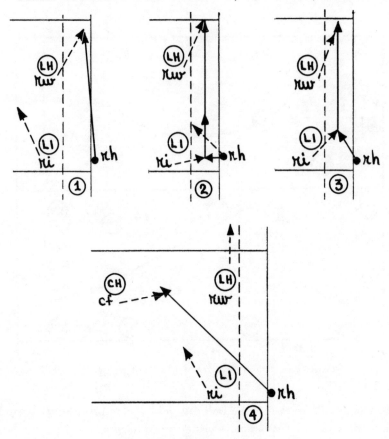

DIAGRAM 15. *Roll-in plays: right halfback.*

More conventional plays for right halfback to try are described here. (Diagram 15 illustrates plays 1, 2, 3, and 4.)

1. *rh* rolls down the alley to *rw*. The roll should be very close to the side line to give *rw* time to dodge by her opponent, LH.

2. *rh* makes a short roll into the alley, almost opposite *ri*. The latter meets the ball in the middle of the alley and returns the pass immediately to *rh* ahead and on her stick side, who drives down the alley to *rw*. This play is not advised for beginners because several players have to handle the ball—and stickwork must be good to assure success of the play.

3. *rh* rolls into the alley and slightly ahead of *ri* who drives down the alley to the stick side of *rw*.

4. *rh* rolls diagonally forward to *cf*. This is a good pass if *ri* and LI (who is marking) stand directly opposite *rh* so that *rh* can roll the ball behind the opposing LI and to the stick side of *cf*.

5. *rh* reverse-rolls back to her own *rb* who should drive the ball down the field or diagonally across the field to the far wing or inner (not illustrated).

Note: If the roll is not sent to *rw* she should not cross the 5-yard line until the ball is finally directed toward her; then she should run into the alley to pick it up.

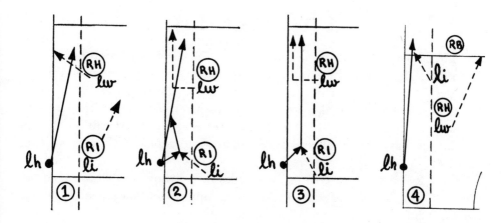

DIAGRAM 16. *Roll-in plays: left halfback.*

The various roll-in passes the left halfback might try are described and illustrated above. (Diagram 16 portrays plays 1, 2, 3, and 4.)

1. *lh* rolls down the middle of the alley to *lw*. On this pass *lw* runs out toward the side line and attempts to pick up the ball on her stick side.

2. *lh* makes a short roll to *li* who meets the ball in the middle of the alley. *lh,* who has come into the alley only a step or two, receives a short hit on her stick side from *li* and immediately passes ahead to *lw*. This is hard to execute successfully and is not recommended for beginners because several players have to handle the ball.

3. *lh* rolls to *li* who meets the ball in the middle of the alley and drives ahead to *lw*. *lw* runs out toward the side line and attempts to pick up the pass on her stick side.

4. *lh* rolls down the alley to *li*. *lw* who has drawn back near *lh* to decoy the opponents races to *li* position.

5. *lh* may roll to *ch*. (See page 58.)

6. *lh* may reverse-roll to *lb* (not illustrated).

Note: The main object of not rolling directly to *lw* is to give *lw* a chance to get across the alley and out to the side line, in order to receive the pass on her right (stick) side. If she does not pick up the ball on her right she cannot pass to her inner or center with a right drive without wasting time in handling the ball and running the chance of losing it to an opponent.

Chapter VI

The Free Hit

A free hit is awarded one team because of certain breaches of the rules by the other. The word "free" indicates that the hit is uncontested and unobstructed. Since a member of the team nearest the spot where a foul has been committed is the one to take the hit, obviously everyone should know how to execute one advantageously. The goalkeeper is excepted; she never takes a free hit for fear that an offense player might intercept it within the striking area.

On a free hit the hitter must always know to whom she should send the hit or to what space she should direct a through pass. She must be sure to place the hit to the stick side of a receiver so that the ball can be relayed or carried on easily (Diagrams 2, 3, and 6). If a foul is called on a defender close to the opponents' circle, an attacking forward should take the hit immediately to keep her own halfbacks from coming up too far and to speed up play. If an attacking forward or halfback is awarded a hit near the circle, she should drive the ball a short distance to a space so that a team member can approach the ball on a run and perhaps drive for goal. If a wing takes a corner or a penalty corner, she should hit the ball hard to the circle edge and to the stick of a receiver so that this player can drive for goal (see page 43). To add body weight to the hit, the hitter should step into the ball to drive it rather than attempting to hit the ball from a standing position.

As with the roll-in, the success of the free hit depends upon how quick and alert all players are on the team, and thus how fast they can get the hit off. The hitter must strike at a motionless ball, may use any legal stroke for the hit, and may not play the ball again until another player has touched it. Everyone remains at least 5 yards away from the hitter. If an opponent is closer than 5 yards at the time the hit is driven, the umpire will not recall the hit if the opposing team does not secure an advantage. As she swings, if the hitter misses the ball and does not make sticks, she may try again.

Whenever a halfback takes a free hit, her two other halfbacks support her and back up the forward line, letting the two fullbacks cover. If this hit occurs near the circle, the opposing fullbacks and center halfback mark the attacking line players closely so that they have less opportunity to drive for goal if the hit is directed their way.

Attacking forwards should be ready to move into a position to receive the ball from the person taking the free hit. Defending forwards, except those actually watching the space or those near the person taking the free hit, should be in a position to receive the ball from their own defense players should the latter intercept the hit. The opposing inner may drop back to try to intercept the hit and then relay it to a member of her line.

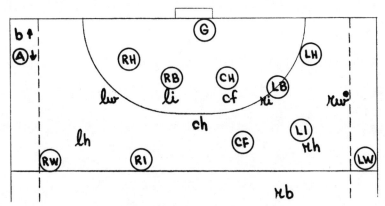

DIAGRAM 17. *Wing free hit near the striking circle.*

FREE HIT SITUATIONS

Diagrams 17-24 and their descriptions illustrate acceptable marking and covering positions of attack and defense players in various free hit situations. Of course, these represent "perfect" places.

DIAGRAM 17. Team A fouls near the circle in wing's territory. Team *b wing* takes the hit in order not to draw her half up too far. (Illustrated by *rw.*)

DEFENSIVE TEAM—A

LB, RB, and CH mark *ri, li,* and *cf* since one of these three forwards is likely to receive the hit.
LH is ready to pick up *rw* after she puts the ball in play.
RH marks *lw* loosely.
LI drops back from her forward line to mark *rh,* since *rw* may direct the hit to her halfback.
CF draws over toward LI to watch *ch.*
Other line players remain near the 25-yard line.
G keeps close to nearer goalpost.

OFFENSIVE TEAM—*b*

rw may pass to *ri,* or *cf* (ahead of them and into the circle, so that they may try to run by opponents to pick up the hit and drive for goal), or to *rh.* A hit to *ch* is not advised.
Forward line players try to keep on line with *rw.*
lh, ch, and *rh* back up their own line.
rb backs up her team since the ball is on her side of the field.
lb covers deep in the center of the field near the center line (not shown).

Note: If *lw* takes a free hit from the other side of the field, *li* will have difficulty fielding the ball quickly, unless she keeps her left shoulder toward the goal and receives the pass well ahead of her or on her right.

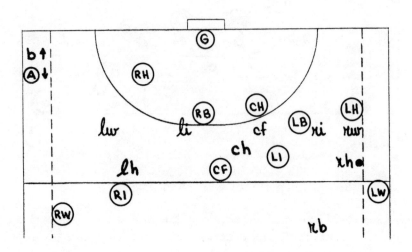

DIAGRAM 18. *Halfback free hit near the 25-yard line.*

DIAGRAM 18. Team A fouls near the 25-yard line Team *b halfback* takes hit. (Illustrated by *rh* taking the hit.)

DEFENSIVE TEAM—A

> RB, CH, and LB mark *li, cf,* and *ri,* since one of these forwards is likely to receive the hit.
> LH marks *rw* as long as the ball is on her side of the field.
> RH covers, watches *lw.*
> LI may drop back out of line to attempt to intercept the free hit.
> CF marks *ch* loosely.
> Other line players keep ahead of CF in anticipation of a ball cleared to them by their defense players.

OFFENSIVE TEAM—b

> *rh* should pass to a teammate who is not marked *(ri, cf, ch).* A pass to *li* or *rw* is not advised.
> *lh* and *ch* back up their own forward line.
> *rb* backs up her team since the ball is on her side of the field.
> *lb* covers deep in the center of the field near the center line (not shown).

Note: If *lh* takes the free hit from approximately the same area on the opposite side of the field, her best pass is either to *li* or *cf.*

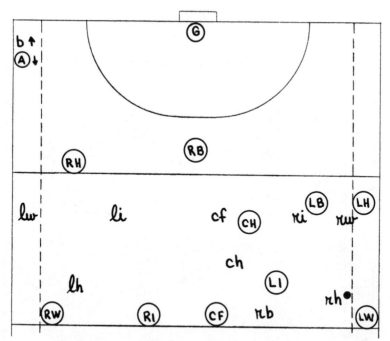

DIAGRAM 19. *Halfback free hit between the 25-yard lines.*

DIAGRAM 19. Team A fouls in wing halfback territory—anywhere between the two 25-yard lines, but not in the alley. Team *b halfback* takes the hit. (Illustrated by *rh* taking the hit.)

DEFENSIVE TEAM—A

> LB marks *ri;* LH marks *rw*—to keep them from receiving the ball.
> CH marks *cf* loosely and attempts to get between *cf* and *ri*.
> RB and RH cover.
> LI may drop back out of her forward line to try to intercept the hit—tries to get between *ch* and *rh*.
> RW, RI, CF keep ahead of LI.
> LW may try to intercept the hit.

OFFENSIVE TEAM—*b*

> *rh* may hit to *rw, ri, cf,* or *ch,* but preferably to *rw* or *ri*.
> *ch* and *rb* back up line; *lh* backs up or covers.
> All members of the forward line keep on line.
> *lb* covers deep in the center near the 25-yard line (not shown).

Note: If *lh* takes the free hit, she may drive to *lw, li,* or possibly to *cf.* RH, in marking *lw,* would not be drawn into the alley. *lw* may await the hit out to the side line in contrast to *rw* who awaits the free hit from her *rh* at the 5-yard line.

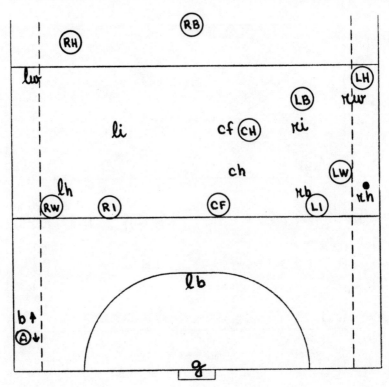

DIAGRAM 20. *Halfback free hit in the alley between the 25-yard lines.*

DIAGRAM 20. Team A fouls in the alley, anywhere between the two 25-yard lines. Team *b wing halfback* takes the hit. (Illustrated by *rh* taking the hit).

DEFENSIVE TEAM—A

> LH marks *rw*—stands in alley. LB marks *ri;* CH marks *cf* loosely.
> RB and RH cover.
> LW may drop out of the forward line to try to intercept the hit— tries to get between *rh* and *ch* to block a direct hit to *ch*.
> CF, LI, RI, and RW play ahead of LW and on line with one another.

OFFENSIVE TEAM—b

> *rh* may hit to *rw, ri,* or *ch.*
> *lw* and *rw* play ahead of the other three forwards in the line.
> *ch* and *rb* back up own forward line.
> *ih* backs up or covers. *lb* covers deep.

Note: This situation is different from Diagram 19 only so far as Team A—LW is concerned. LW, if she intercepts the hit, may carry the ball out into the alley or relay the hit to her forward line.

   If *lh* takes the hit she may drive to *lw* or *li*. RW may drop out of her line to attempt to intercept the hit.

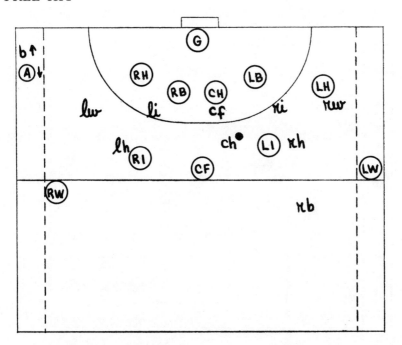

DIAGRAM 21. *Center halfback free hit near the striking circle.*

DIAGRAM 21. Team A fouls in the center of the field near the striking circle. Team *b center halfback* takes the hit.

DEFENSIVE TEAM—A

> RB, CH, and LB mark *li, cf* and *ri.*
> RH and LH play near their opposing wings until the direction of the ball is known. They may then either watch the wing, cover, or back up their own line.
> RI and LI may drop back from their own forward line to mark *lh* and *rh* loosely in case *ch* should drive the ball to either one. This is not likely because *ch* usually sends the hit toward the goal.
> RW, CF, and LW play near the 25-yard line.

OFFENSIVE TEAM—b

> *ch* may hit to an opening near either of the inners or *cf.* A short hit is advised, and should be directed to the proper side of the receiver. *li* and *cf* should keep their left shoulders toward the goal, so that they will be in a good position for a drive to goal. Inners move out from the center to draw opposing defense away.
> Wings play outside the circle.
> *rh* and *lh* back up their own line.
> *rb* covers.
> *lb* covers deep in the center of the field near the center line (not shown).

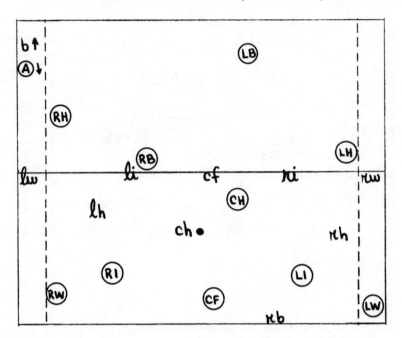

DIAGRAM 22. *Center halfback free hit between the 25-yard lines.*

DIAGRAM 22. Team A fouls in the center of the field anywhere between the two 25-yard lines. Team *b center halfback* takes the hit.

DEFENSIVE TEAM—A

> CH marks *of* loosely—keeps between *of* and *ch,* tries to intercept the hit.
> RB marks *li.*
> LB covers deep. If the pass is to *ri* or *rw,* LB comes up immediately to assist LH.
> LH watches *ri* and *rw.*
> RH marks *lw* loosely.

The forward line members may keep ahead and on line with one another. However RI and LI may drop back (as illustrated) to watch *lh* and *rh* and perhaps be of assistance in relaying the ball to their wings if their backfield intercepts the hit.

OFFENSIVE TEAM—*b*

> *ch* may hit to anyone on the forward line and may even use her halfbacks, though the latter is not advised.
> Forward line players keep well ahead of the ball and on line with one another.
> *lh* and *rh* back up their own forward line. *rb* covers.
> *lb* covers deep in the center of the field about in striking circle area (not shown).

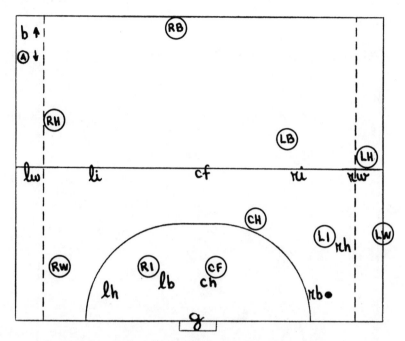

DIAGRAM 23. *Fullback free hit near the goal line, outside the circle.*

DIAGRAM 23. Team A fouls near the goal line outside the striking circle. Team *b fullback* takes the hit. (Illustrated by *rb* taking the hit.)

DEFENSIVE TEAM—A

    LW keeps near the side line to try to intercept a hit to *rh* or *rw*.
    LI tries to intercept—keeps near *rh*.
    RI, RW, and CF keep on line with one another.
    LB and LH mark *ri* and *rw* since the ball is on their side of the field.
    CH keeps between *cf* and *rb* to try to intercept the ball.
    RH and RB cover.

OFFENSIVE TEAM— *b*

    rb may drive to *rh* or hard up the alley to *rw*.
    ch marks CF since CF is in the circle.
    lb marks RI since RI is in the circle.
    lh watches RW, ready to back up her line if hit is successful.
    rh tries to keep free for a pass from *rb*.
    Forward line stays out near the 25-yard line.

Note: It is suggested that the fullback rather than the halfback take the free hit from this area because, if the hit is successful, the halfback immediately will be in a position to back up her own line. The fullback must mark her inner as soon as she completes the hit. If *lb* takes the hit on the opposite side, the drive should go to *lh* or to *lw*.

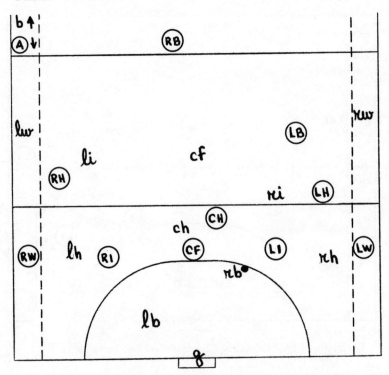

DIAGRAM 24. *Fullback free hit from the edge of the striking circle.*

DIAGRAM 24. Team A fouls in the circle. Team *b fullback* takes the hit from any place in the circle. (Illustrated by *rb* hitting near center of circle line.)

DEFENSIVE TEAM—A

Because of the long distance between the ball and Team *b's* goal, the defensive halfbacks—RH, CH, LH—can afford to neglect their own opponents on the line in an attempt to intercept the hit. Thus, if RB and LB cover, RH, LH, and CH can mark *lh, rh,* and *ch* loosely.

Line players keep ahead of their defense and must be alert to keep on side after *rb* hits the ball.

OFFENSIVE TEAM—b

rb may drive to either the right or left—to halfbacks, wings, or inners. *lh, rh,* and *ch*—who are neglecting their opposing forwards—play ahead of *rb* and try to keep free so that they can pick up the ball.

lb covers. *g* keeps in line with the ball.

Line members stay beyond the 25-yard line and watch for a long drive from *rb*. *ri* plays back of teammate hoping to intercept the hit.

Note: If Team *b* loses the ball the players are not in too precarious a situation, because *rb*, who follows up her initial drive, may force Team A forwards offside unless they drop back in line with the ball.

CORNER HIT SITUATIONS

Corner hits are free hits from a designated spot on the goal line or side line. They are taken by a member of the attacking team and are of two types. One—the ordinary corner or "long" corner—is awarded the attacking team whenever the ball goes over the goal line not between the goal posts (1) off the stick or person of the defending goalkeeper or (2) off the stick of any other member of the defending team behind the 25-yard line or (3) whenever an attacker hits the ball outside the striking circle and it glances off the stick of a defender in the striking circle and goes into the goal. The hit on this corner is taken from a point on the side or goal line within 5 yards of the corner of the field on the side where the ball went out of bounds. If the ball goes off the field between the goalposts on a corner award, the attacking team may choose either side for the corner. The second type of corner is the penalty or "short" corner. This hit is awarded whenever, in the umpire's opinion, any player of the defending team intentionally sends the ball over the goal line not between the posts. For the penalty corner the hit is taken from a point on the goal line not less than 10 yards from the nearer goalpost, on whichever side of the field the attacking team chooses.

An attacking wing generally takes the hit. On either type of corner all members of the attacking team except the hitter must be outside the circle in the field of play. Six members of the defending team must be behind their own goal line; the others must remain beyond the nearer 25-yard line. These positions must be observed until the ball has been touched by a player other than the hitter or has gone out of the striking circle. On either corner no player may be closer than 5 yards to the ball, and no player may shoot for goal unless an attacker has stopped the ball on the ground (not necessarily motionless), or unless the ball has touched the person or stick of a defender. The hitter may stand in any position behind or on the goal or side line; the ball, however, must be on the line and placed according to rule.

Diagrams 25-27 which follow show player positions on corners and penalty corners. Since any six defending players must remain behind the goal line until the ball is hit, the illustrations show fullbacks, halfbacks, and goalkeeper in this position. Some coaches prefer to have the defending center forward behind the goal line so that she can rush out after the hit to mark the opposing (and attacking) center halfback. In this case the defending halfback on the side where the hit is not taken can go out to the 25-yard line until the hit is completed.

On all corners the four attacking players stand around the circle, left shoulders leading in the direction of the goal mouth and sticks on the ground. In this position each is ready to stop the ball and immediately shoot for goal should the hit be directed her way. The stick on the ground also functions as a target at which the hitter can aim. The defending players behind the goal line generally try to stand opposite the attackers for which they are responsible—on their stick sides.

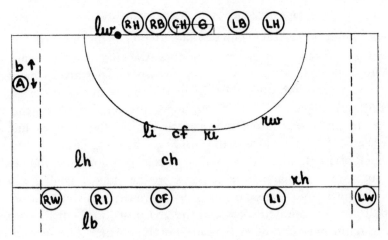

DIAGRAM 25. *Start of a penalty corner by left wing.*

DIAGRAM 25. Team A fouls within the circle. Team *b left wing* takes the hit. *Penalty Corner*—placement of players before *lw* hits the ball.

DEFENSIVE TEAM—A

RB, CH, and LB stand behind goal line opposite *li, cf,* and *ri* respectively—ready to dash out as the ball is hit into the circle.

RH stands 5 yards from *lw*—ready to mark *lw* after she puts the ball in play. G stands within goal mouth.

LH stands opposite *rw*—ready to dash out to mark *rw* loosely.

Five line players space themselves at the 25-yard line until the hit is completed.

OFFENSIVE TEAM—b

lw stands on the goal line 10 yards from the goal post.

li, cf, ri, and *rw* stand at the circle—ready to receive the hit (Diagram 3).

ch backs up whoever is to receive the hit (predetermined by signal from *lw*).

lh is on line with *ch;* both back up the line players.

rh remains near the 25-yard line—ready to back up should *ri* or *rw* receive the hit.

lb covers near the 25-yard line.

rb covers deep in the center of the field between the 25-yard and center lines (not shown).

Note: When *lw* takes the penalty corner, RB, RH, and CH are at a disadvantage for clearing the ball to the side since they will have to clear with a right drive; if *rw* takes the hit, LB and LH are in excellent positions for clearing. (Wings who take the corner should look to a receiver *before* they swing.)

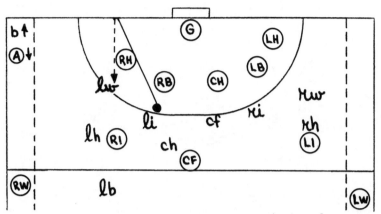

DIAGRAM 26. *Positions of players just after a penalty corner hit.*

DIAGRAM 26. *Penalty Corner Hit*—approximate positions of players just after the hit is directed to *li* or *cf*. (After a corner, players are in similar positions.)

DEFENSIVE TEAM—A

> RB rushes into the circle to mark *li* on the stick side.
>
> LB rushes in to mark *ri*. If she marks on the stick side, she permits *ri* a direct line to the goal; LB should mark directly in front of *ri*.
>
> LH covers; she watches *rw*.
>
> RH marks *lw* as she enters the circle.
>
> CH marks *cf*. CH rushes in front of *cf* to block her direct line to the goal.
>
> G shifts her position as the ball shifts within the circle.
>
> RI drops back from her line and toward the circle. She is ready to tackle *lh* or *ch* if either intercepts a clear from the defenders.
>
> LI drops back slightly in case the ball shifts to her side. She watches *rh*.
>
> CF, RW, and LW remain near 25-yard line. Wings play ahead of CF.

OFFENSIVE TEAM—*b*

> *lw* runs inside the circle to an onside position.
>
> *li* stops the ball on the circle. She may pass ahead of *cf* or *ri*, or she may shoot for goal. The other forwards keep in line with the receiver.
>
> *ch* backs up *li*, who has received the pass—she tries to keep in the area between *li* and *cf*.
>
> *lh* draws toward the circle to back up her wing or inner. *lh* may also intercept a clear to the side from her opponents.
>
> *lb* covers near the 25-yard line.
>
> *rb* covers deep in the center of the field between the 25-yard line and center line (not shown).

> *Note:* If forwards miss the ball, *ch* is ready to field the ball and either pass ahead to the line or dribble to the circle and shoot. *ri* is alert to rush clearing shots by the opponents.

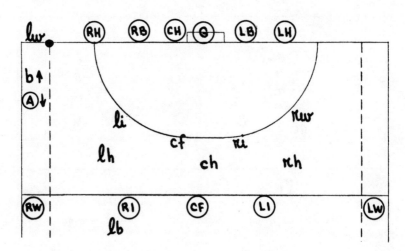

DIAGRAM 27. *Start of a corner by left wing.*

DIAGRAM 27. Team A unintentionally hits the ball over the goal line on the defending team's right side. Team *b left wing* takes the hit. *Corner*—placement of players before *lw* hits the ball.

DEFENSIVE TEAM—A

> RB, CH, and LB stand behind goal line opposite *li, cf,* and *ri,* respectively, ready to dash in the circle to mark these players or to pick up the ball when the hit is completed.
> RH stands behind the goal line near the edge of the circle to be close to *lw.* G stands in goal mouth.
> LH stands behind the goal line opposite *rw.*
>
> *Note:* If *rw* takes the hit, LH stands behind the goal line near the edge of the circle to mark *rw* when she enters the field; RH stands behind the line opposite *lw,* ready to mark *lw* closely when the hit is completed.

OFFENSIVE TEAM—*b*

> *lw* stands on the goal line 5 yards from the corner.
> *li, cf, ri,* and *rw* space themselves around the striking circle—*cf* opposite the nearer goalpost rather than opposite the center of the goal, because a corner hit travels a greater distance than a penalty corner hit. These line players are ready to receive the ball on the edge of the circle.
> *ch* backs up *cf* or *ri,* whoever is to receive the hit. (In the illustration, *ch* backs up *cf.*)
> *lh* is ready to back up *li* if she receives the hit.
> *rh* is ready to back up *ri* or *rw,* or to intercept a clear from the defense.
> *lb* covers near the 25-yard line since the ball is on her side of the field.
> *rb* covers deep on her side, between the 25-yard and center lines and in the middle of the field (not shown).

Note: If *rw* takes the hit, the remaining line players move more to the right on the circle, *cf* opposite the nearer goalpost. *ch* backs up *cf* or *li*. *rh* is ready to back up *ri*. *lh* may back up; she is ready to intercept a clear. *rb* covers near the 25-yard line. *lb* covers deep.

When *lw* takes the corner, RB, RH, and CH are at a disadvantage for clearing the ball to the side since they have to clear with a right drive; if *rw* takes the hit, LB and LH are in a much better spot for clearing shots.

FIGURE 16. *Bully*—Players standing squarely, hands well apart, heads almost over the ball.

Chapter VII

The Bully

To bully, two players face each other squarely (feet astride and pointed toward the sidelines), right hands halfway down the stick, heads down and almost over the ball, and stick extended out in front and on the ground. The ball is placed on the line (center line, 25-yard line, or imaginary line) between the blades of the two sticks. To start the bully, each of the two players raises the stick slightly and then strikes alternately three times first the ground on her own side of the ball and the face of her opponent's stick. Then either is free to hit the ball. The player who executes the technique ("ground-sticks-ground-sticks-ground-sticks") faster completes the bully first and can immediately play the ball. The methods she may use to secure possession of the ball after she completes the bully and the possible action which may result are outlined below. For illustrative purposes, the center foward is selected.

1. Center forward reverses her stick and hits the ball back to her center halfback who immediately passes the ball to either inner. To reverse the stick, the player turns it quickly in her grasp from right to left. The right hand is under the stick so that the right wrist can do the work. The stick merely slips in the left hand. Instead of reversing her stick, center forward may lift it from the ground and her opponent may inadvertently hit the ball back to center halfback.

2. Center forward hits the ball hard against her opponent's stick and forces the ball through her opponent. If the ball becomes wedged between the two sticks, center forward steps with her right foot so that her weight comes behind her stick (as in tackling), exerts a pressure against the ball, and pulls it up over her opponent's stick.

3. Center forward passes to right inner by pushing the ball between her opposing center forward's right foot and stick. This tactic may be used if the opponent keeps her right hand high up on the stick.

4. Center forward pulls the ball toward her as she moves back quickly, steps to the left and passes to left inner, or drives to left wing; or pulls the ball toward her with a reversed stick, and then steps back to the right and passes to right inner or wing. Try these against an inexperienced player.

Each time a bully is awarded all members of both teams must be on their own side of the field. Of course, since the two players who take the bully face each other as well as the side lines, one foot of each player and her stick will be in opponent's territory.

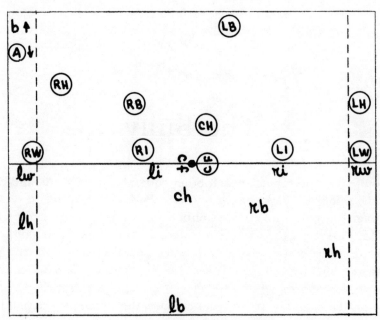

DIAGRAM 28. *Start of a center bully.*

CENTER BULLY

Center bully occurs at the beginning of the game and of each half, and after a goal is scored. This bully is taken in the middle of center line.

DIAGRAM 28. The lineup of members of both teams as two center forwards execute a center bully. On each team:

Inners are closer to the center forward than they are to the wings; wings are out in the alley.

Center halfback backs up the center forward on the stick side of the opponent.

Right fullback is almost on a line with center halfback, because the ball most likely will be hit to her side of the field (natural drive), and is on the stick side of inner.

Left halfback is on the stick side of the opposing right wing, thus plays out in the alley.

Right halfback is on the stick side of the opposing left wing. She plays near the 5-yard line rather than in the alley.

Left fullback covers deep in the center of the field near 25-yard line. She comes up immediately in order to take the opposing right inner if the ball goes to her side of the field.

Note: Wing halfbacks should never be drawn toward the center of the field just after a center bully has been completed; they should allow the center halfbacks and the fullbacks to take care of the ball. Very likely the ball will be directed to the wings where the wing halfbacks should be.

25-YARD LINE BULLY

The game is restarted with a bully at the 25-yard line in these instances: if an attacker within the circle sends the ball over the goal line, not between the goal posts, or outside the circle, sends the ball over the goal line; if a defender who is *beyond* the 25-yard line unintentionally, in the umpire's opinion, sends the ball over the goal line; and if the ball crosses the goal line, not between the posts, off the sticks of two opponents. In each of these cases the bully is taken at a spot on the 25-yard line opposite the place where the ball went out of bounds. Diagram 29 shows the offense and defense positions for a 25-yard line bully.

PENALTY BULLY

A penalty bully is awarded if a member of the defending team fouls in the striking circle when the attacking team might have scored a goal had not the foul occurred. The bully is played by the defender who fouled and by any player selected by the attacking team. The ball is placed on a spot 5 yards in front of the center of the goal line. If the goalkeeper is the defender she loses her kicking privilege during the bully and may not remove her goalie pads to participate in the bully. All members of both teams must keep out of the play and must remain beyond nearer 25-yard line.

A penalty goal or goal results, or the bully is taken again, or the bully is over, depending upon the following:

1. If G kicks the ball, makes sticks, or makes any other foul, a penalty goal is awarded the offense.
2. If either G or *cf* sends the ball between the goal posts, a goal is awarded the offense.
3. If G gets ball out of the striking circle, bully is over.
4. If *cf* puts ball over goal line not between the posts, or if *cf* fouls, bully is over.
5. If G puts ball over goal line not between the posts, bully is taken again.
6. If the ball goes over the goal line not between the posts off the sticks of G and *cf,* bully is taken again.
7. If *cf* and G foul simultaneously, or if they bully improperly, bully is taken again.
8. If there is interference by any other player, bully is taken again.

After a penalty goal or a goal, the game is resumed with a bully in the center of the field; otherwise the game is restarted at the center of the nearer 25-yard line.

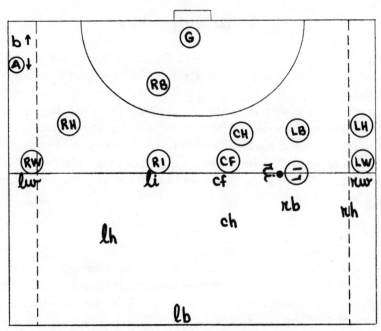

DIAGRAM 29. *Inner bully at the 25-yard line.*

DIAGRAM 29. Bully at the 25-yard line. Inners take the bully. (Illustrated by LI and *ri* bullying.)

DEFENSIVE TEAM—A

CF draws over toward her LI, anticipating a short pass.
RI draws closer to CF.
LW stands in the alley; RW in or close to her alley. (If the bully occurs nearer the center of the field, wings will be closer to inners.)
LB backs up the bully.
CH and LH back up their line players.
RH and RB cover.
G is alert to shift her position when the direction of the ball is determined.

OFFENSIVE TEAM—*b*

Line players play opposite opposing line players, on their stick side.
rb backs up the bully.
ch and *rh* back up their line players. *lh* covers.
lb covers deep in the center of the field near the center line.

Note: If the wings take the bully in the alley, the wing halfbacks back up the bully, supported by the nearer fullbacks and center halfbacks; if the center forwards take the bully in the center of the 25-yard line, the defense players back up and cover as they are illustrated and explained for Diagram 28.

Chapter VIII
Defense Play

Halfbacks and fullbacks in defense play synchronize their tactics and function as a unit whether their team is on attack or on defense. On attack, halfbacks back up (support) the line players who have the ball or fullbacks back up halfbacks with the ball. On attack one or two defense players cover. When they are on the defensive, backs tackle their opposing forward or backfield player who has the ball, mark (guard) their opponents who do not have the ball so that they have less chance of receiving a pass, and cover. On defense, backs must be ready to shift positions to tackle or mark their teammates' opposing forwards whenever their teammates are left behind and cannot recover their positions before the ball nears the scoring area.

Whenever a player marks, backs up, or covers she knows where the ball is every second of play and tries to anticipate the moves of her teammates as well as of the opponents. She always maintains a position of readiness. Here this means that she carries her weight forward rather than settling back on her heels, keeps her stick down, and points her toes in the direction of her goal. When backing up or covering she can readily watch the blade of the opponent's stick to get the angle of the pass. The ball goes in whatever direction the blade of the stick faces when it contacts the ball. A player who can judge where an opponent will send a pass has an advantage over the others and can shift into a position to intercept the ball and place her team immediately on attack. To make it difficult for the defense, clever stick handlers never divulge the intended direction of the pass.

Details follow on the tactics of marking, backing up, and covering, and on how and when to shift positions to help backfield players who are left behind. For best results in controlling the opponents' action, all backfield players should know what is required to play each position.

MARKING

To mark an opponent means to be close enough to her to prevent her from receiving a pass or to immediately tackle her if she does get the ball. Both forwards and defense players mark, but the defense does so much more marking that it is considered a defense responsibility. No player marks the entire game —only when an opponent or her neighbor is likely to receive the ball. Basically, a team's defense is set up so that each halfback and each fullback has a forward on the opposing team for whom she is responsible. When she marks this player she never wanders more than a yard from her, keeps between her and the goal, and, unless she is the left halfback, usually plays on the stick side of the opponent. (The left halfback must have the opposing right wing slightly to her nonstick side so that she will be in a better position to intercept passes to this wing.) Briefly, left halfback marks her opposing right wing, left fullback the right inner, center halfback the center forward, right fullback the left inner, and right halfback the left wing. All defense players mark closely in the striking area—they seldom dash forward to intercept the ball in this area. On a corner hit the five defensive players are in a position to mark all five forwards as soon as the hit is completed. This is one of the few times an ideal situation occurs, that is, when all backfield players are available to mark the opponents for whom they are responsible.

From the above, defense players may gather that they are responsible for line players only. This is not always the case. Though they do not mark these players, they are sometimes answerable for the actions of a defense player who is opposite their position on the field. Fullbacks rarely, if ever, tackle their opposing backs as the inner playing against the back should immediately tackle back if she loses the ball. It is near the edge of the circle that the wing halfback may be called upon to take care of her opposing wing halfback. A defending wing halfback must tackle one that is attacking at the moment she is to shoot for goal or pass off to one of the inside forwards. An attacking wing halfback or center halfback must tackle her opposite defense if she has secured the ball and is attempting to pass the ball unmolested to her forwards. The attacking players want to keep the ball on the attack and even if the defending team does maintain possession of the ball, these halfbacks have time to recover their defensive positions before a really dangerous situation can arise. It is always best to keep the ball on the attack.

If opposing line members stand still to await the ball instead of moving continually and making spaces for a pass, a defense player can mark loosely —play close to but back of the forward instead of between the forward and the goal—and play an intercepting type of game. This tactic should be employed only when opponents are weak players, otherwise the would-be interceptor may get left behind too often and weaken her team's defense.

Line members mark loosely on free hits and roll-ins. (Refer to diagrams on the free hit and the roll-in.) In particular the inners, not the fullbacks, always mark the opposing inners on a roll-in between the two 25-yard lines, in order not to bring the fullback out of position when the ball is on her side of the field.

BACKING UP

To back up means to support and play close behind the teammate who has the ball in the hope that, if she loses the ball, the one who is behind may be able to pick it up and return it to a member of her own team. Immediately the forward line players (or perhaps the halfbacks) have obtained possession of the ball and are carrying it toward the goal; the defense players who were marking or covering are thrown on the attack and must back up their teammates. In this shift the fullback on the side of the field where the ball is not plays deep in covering position. The backing up must take place quickly. Too wide a gap between backfield players and their own forwards is disastrous; it means that the backfield players are weak on attack or too tired to support the forward line. Backfield players who give their forwards the proper support shift up and back—from back-up position to cover position— depending upon which side of the field the ball is played. If their attacking forwards lose the ball to an opponent, and if the back-up player-defender misses a tackle, she may be left behind. If she cannot recover quickly, her teammates, now thrown on defense, may have to shift positions to stop the attacker with the ball or to mark the ball-carrier's neighbors.

Near the striking circle all halfbacks on attack back up closely. If their forwards are close to the goal these halfbacks hold themselves near the edge of the circle and try to intercept a defender's clearing shot. In this position they may have an opportunity to shoot for goal themselves. Attacking wings assist the halfbacks in backing up inside forwards around the circle; they pick up clears that are near the goal line and drive the ball back into play. Halfbacks who back up near the 25-yard line and near the striking area seldom hit the ball out to their wings when they get it. A pass to their own inside forwards is preferable, since these players can score more readily because of their central position in the scoring area (Diagrams 2 and 7).

COVERING

To cover means to play deep, on the side of the field away from the activity with the ball. Wing halfbacks and fullbacks cover, the fullbacks often much deeper than the halfbacks. The covering defense players on their right-hand side of the field play more towards the center of the field in order to be on the stick side of two very active opposing forwards, the left inner and center forward. Those covering on the left do not station themselves quite so far in towards the center of the field because they are on the stick side of all opposing line players, except the right wing. One fullback always covers in a deep position; this player is closer to the goal her team is defending than any other teammate except the goalkeeper. This deep fullback is at least 25 yards behind any other covering player. Often this back can intercept a long pass the opponents have directed up the center of the field and, by so doing, put her team on attack.

Fullbacks always function as a pair—the movement up the field or back of one affecting the movement of the other. Of course, the fullback who plays up is nearer to the action of the game. Where the ball is being played determines the movement of the fullbacks. When the ball shifts from one side of the field to the other, the back who has been up drops to the covering position and, at the same time, the back who has been playing deep starts up. A somewhat similar movement occurs with the wing halfbacks, except that no halfback plays as deep in the field as the fullback. Wing halfbacks are often in a position to assist the fullback who cannot get up the field fast enough to take her inner when the play shifts from defense to offense. Wing halfbacks have to synchronize their play with that of the two fullbacks. The former must have an understanding with the latter about when a wing half-back should move in from the side of the field, either to tackle the opposing inner who has the ball or mark her if the center forward or other inner has the ball.

PLAY SITUATIONS

At certain times backfield players must move in quickly to take over the responsibilities of teammates who have been left behind, or the attackers will reach the scoring area unimpeded. This shifting to take over a teammate's attacker occurs only as a last resort—when the defense is sure that the team-mate left behind cannot recover her own position or cannot tackle back on the ball-carrier in time to help defend in the strategic area. For example, if the attacker dodges by the defender in midfield, a covering fullback does not immediately rush in to tackle the ball-carrier; she holds back to give her team-mate a chance to tackle back on the ball-carrier first. If the left-behind team-mate does recover and can spoil the attacker's progress with the ball or force her to pass, then, of course, any necessity for shifts among the defenders has been avoided. On the other hand, if the attacking forwards have the ball near the circle when the defender has been left behind, the covering fullback dare not hesitate regarding her action. She either tackles the ball-carrier or marks the free forward. For example, if the wing halfback is left behind and the attacking wing with the ball approaches the circle, the fullback on that side of the field shifts over to tackle the wing and the covering backfield player shifts to mark the inner who has been left free. Diagrams 30-31 show this situation. In both of the illustrated situations, the fullbacks force the play at scoring territory. (See pages 86 and 87). Diagrams 30 through 36 illustrate defense play when backfield players have been left behind. For reasons of clarity, so that movements of players and the ball within the field can be conveyed, only the actions of the defensive halfbacks, fullbacks, and goal-keeper and the five attacking forwards are pictured and explained.

The center halfback is never involved in any shift to take care of holes in the defense caused by players being left behind. She never leaves her center forward to tackle another forward with the ball. She, however, does find her-self in the awkward position of being left behind, and her defending left full-back takes over the attacking center forward when this occurs. The left full-back tackles the attacking center forward because she is on the attacker's stick side. When this happens the defending left halfback comes in to mark the fullback's right inner (see Diagrams 32 and 33).

Whenever two defense are left behind and cannot recover, covering de-fenders move in to take care of the contingency. The three inside forwards must be marked; these are the most dangerous attackers. Hence the covering backs watch and mark these players, leaving the wings unmolested or unguarded until they reach the scoring area. For example, if a wing has the ball when two defenders are left behind, the defending teammates watch the inside forwards until the wing nears the circle. Then the nearest defense player shifts over to tackle her and the remaining defenders shift to mark the unmarked forwards nearest the ball. Other situations where two defenders are left behind and inside forwards have the ball are described and illustrated in Diagrams 34 and 35.

When fullbacks, in the circle area especially, miss tackles and are left behind, a shot for goal is inevitable unless someone hinders the forwards. If left fullback is left behind, left halfback who is on the stick side of the attacking right inner is the player to move in to take her. If right fullback is left behind, left halfback again is the player involved; it would be unlikely that right halfback could tackle since the attacking inner is on her nonstick side and since she is marking her left wing loosely because the ball is on her side of the field. In either case—whether right inner or left inner with the ball has passed by the defending back—the goalkeeper probably comes out to tackle before the left halfback can shift to help. Left halfback may be able to spoil the inners' chances to score a rebound (see Diagram 36).

Any player who is left behind recovers as quickly as possible to the goal side of the opponents. Often the recovering defender can pick up her own attacking player right away. Certainly she resumes her position and duties if her own team is put on attack. When she recovers to the circle, however, she must not hamper the work of the other defense members who perhaps have shifted to mark the free players and she must not block the view of the goalkeeper. Recovering players generally remain out toward the side edge of the circle to receive clears from the goalkeeper and drive the ball up the field to start their team on attack. When the circle area is congested, it is better not to rush back into the center of the playing area because the recoverer may hinder instead of help (see Diagrams 33 and 36).

The goalkeeper is an important link in the defense setup described in the above paragraphs. She always faces the play and often helps members of her team, especially those recovering, by calling out who should shift to mark or tackle in a tight situation where left-behind players are out of the immediate picture. She can tell at a glance, as the attackers draw near her area, whether she should come out from the mouth of the goal to tackle the forward with the ball or take the pass or the free forward. If she decides to come out she calls "Mine!" in a voice loud enough to be heard by her defending teammates. Once she calls her play and comes out the other defense players watch their opponents carefully and the covering player protects the goal. All defense players assist her by clearing the ball when received up to their own forwards.

A goalkeeper is only as good as the defense in front of her. If she continually has to try to stop shots from forwards who are permitted to shoot for goal unmolested, she has a difficult time. If her view of the ball is continually blocked by careless defenders, her defense breaks down. When halfbacks, fullbacks, and goalkeeper work together, the last line of defense is a strong unit.

In sum, for good defensive teamwork players must recognize the abilities of their teammates to recover, for too much shifting among backfield players weakens team play. Mutual understanding—sensing when to tackle or mark and when to hold back to give those left behind an opportunity to recover—and cooperative efforts between backs and goalkeeper will make it difficult for the attackers to penetrate the goal.

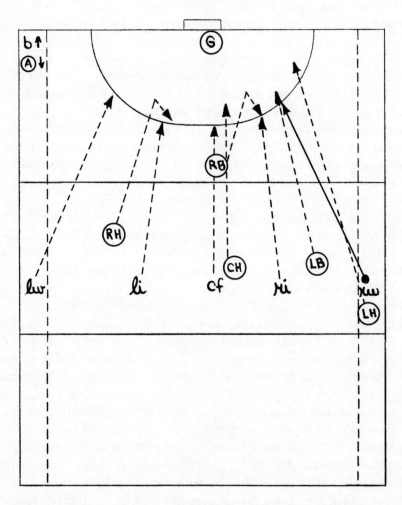

DIAGRAM 30. *Defense play when LH is left behind in the center of the field and* rw *takes the ball to the circle.*

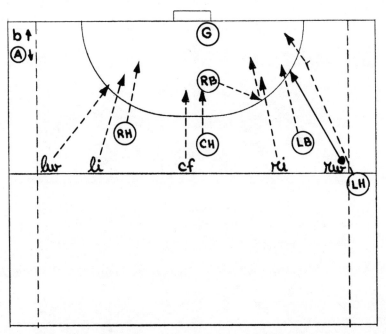

DIAGRAM 31. *Defense play when LH is left behind at the 25-yard line.*

DIAGRAMS 30 and 31. Team A LH tackles Team *b rw* near the center of the field (30) or near the 25-yard line (31) and misses the tackle. LH is left behind. *rw* continues on with the ball. (Action of backfield players same for 30 and 31.)

BACKFIELD PLAYERS—A

> LB tackles *rw* at the edge of the circle, because LH has not been able to recover in time.
> LH runs back to her position in the circle where she can pick up *rw* and help clear.
> CH marks *cf* throughout.
> RB, who has been covering, marks *ri* in the circle.
> RH, who also has been covering, marks *li* in the circle.
> G moves in line with the ball.

FORWARDS—*b*

> *rw* dodges LH and continues to the circle with the ball.
> Line players keep up with *rw*.

Note: If RH tackles *lw* in a similar situation and is left behind, RB takes *lw* when she reaches the circle (if RH has not been able to recover). RH runs back to her position in the circle where she can pick up *lw*. In the circle CH marks *cf,* LB marks *li,* and LH marks *ri.*

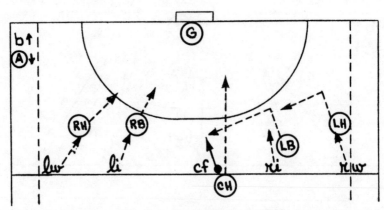

DIAGRAM 32. *Defense play approaching the circle when CH misses a tackle and is left behind.*

DIAGRAM 32. Team *b cf* with the ball dodges Team A CH at the 25-yard line. CH is left behind.

BACKFIELD PLAYERS—A

LB shifts over to take *cf,* since she is near the scoring area.
LH draws in from the side of the field to mark *ri.*
CH recovers to goal side of *cf* as quickly as possible.
RB and RH mark *li* and *lw* loosely.

FORWARDS—*b*

cf dodges by CH. She may pass to *ri* or *li.*
ri and *li* keep on line with *cf.*
rw and *lw* are prepared for interceptions and clears from the backfield players.

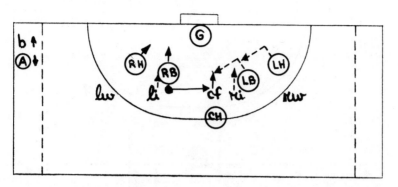

DIAGRAM 33. *Defense play in the circle when CH misses a tackle and is left behind.*

DIAGRAM 33. In the striking circle Team *b cf* receives a short pass from *li*. Team A CH tackles *cf* and misses the tackle. CH is left behind.

BACKFIELD PLAYERS—A

> CH who has missed the tackle stays out of the circle to watch for clears.
> LB shifts over to take *cf*.
> LH shifts over to take *ri*, leaving *rw* free.
> RB marks *li* closely.
> RH watches *lw* and keeps herself free to pick up a clear.
> G lines up with the ball.
>
> *Note:* If *cf* is very close to the goal, G takes her; therefore a shift by LB and LH is not called for.

FORWARDS—*b*

> *li* passes to *cf* in the circle. *cf* gets by CH. She should shoot for goal. Other forwards keep alert for the play.

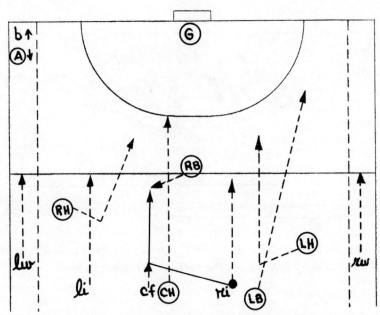

DIAGRAM 34. *Defense play when LB and CH are left behind and* cf *takes the ball down the field.*

DIAGRAM 34. Team A LB tackles Team *b ri* who successfully passes to *cf.* LB is left behind. *cf* gets by her opposing CH. CH is left behind.

BACKFIELD PLAYERS—A

LH crosses over to take *ri* who may receive the ball back from *cf.*

RB covering in the center of the field comes up to tackle *cf* because she realizes that her CH cannot recover in time to make the tackle.

RH moves in to mark *li.*

LB runs back to watch *rw* and back up LH. LB may have to tackle *rw* if she receives the ball.

CH runs straight back to cover on the goal side of *cf.*

FORWARDS—b

ri passes the ball to her *cf.*

cf may keep the ball (as illustrated) or pass back to *ri* or pass to *li.*

ri and *li* keep on a line with *cf.*

rw and *lw* may play slightly ahead of the ball (but must be careful not to be offside) in anticipation of a long diagonal pass from *cf* or *inners.*

Note: It may appear that, when LH draws over to *ri* and leaves *rw* free, there is an excellent opening for a pass to *rw* who can dribble down the field. Experience has proved that LH can get back before the wing nears the circle or can break up the wing's progress with a job or right cut. It is not likely that the forward with the ball will pass until a defense player forces her to do so.

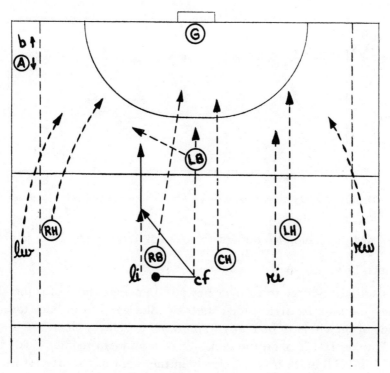

DIAGRAM 35. *Defense play when RB and CH are left behind and* li *takes the ball down the field.*

DIAGRAM 35. By means of a triangular pass—*li* to *cf* to *li*—Team *b* gets by two Team A defense players, RB and CH. Both are left behind. *li* continues with the ball.

Backfield Players—A

LB in covering position waits to see whether RB can get back in time to tackle *li*. RB does not get back so LB tackles *li* near the circle.
LH marks *ri*.
RH, since she is on the nonstick side of the ball-carrier, marks *lw*.
RB and CH try to recover on the goal side of their opponents. CH is in the better position to pick up *cf*.
G moves in line with the ball.

Forwards—*b*

li passes to *cf*, thereby dodging RB; *cf* dodges CH by returning the pass to *li*. *li* continues on with the ball.
cf, ri, and *li* keep on line with one another.
rw and *lw* may play slightly ahead of the ball (but must be careful not to be offside), hoping for a long diagonal pass toward either of the alleys.

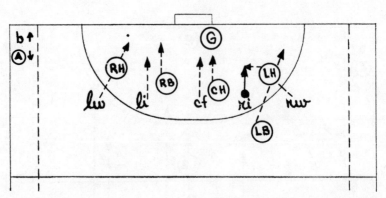

DIAGRAM 36. *Defense play in the circle when LB misses a tackle and is left behind.*

DIAGRAM 36.   Team *b ri* dodges Team A LB in the circle. LB is left behind.

BACKFIELD PLAYERS—A

LB should not try to recover her position since the ball is too close to the goal and the area is too congested. She should run back toward the side of the circle to be ready to mark *rw* or relay a clear.

LH takes *ri*. LH is on the stick side of *ri* and can readily tackle her.

CH and RB mark *cf* and *li* closely in the event of a short pass from *ri* to *cf* or *li*.

RH marks *lw* loosely.

G lines up with the play.

Note: If *ri* is very close to the goal, G takes her.

FORWARDS—b

ri dodges LB at the edge of the circle. She may either drive for goal or send a short pass to *cf* or *li*.

Other forwards keep on line with *ri*.

Note: If *li* has the ball on the other side of the field and RB tackles her and is left behind, LH crosses over to mark or tackle *li,* because she is in a much better position to do so than RH who is on the nonstick side of *li*. LH must be careful not to block G's view. RB remains out of the goal area, ready to relay clears. CH and LB mark *cf* and *ri* closely.   In this play *rw* remains unmarked.

Chapter IX

Goaltending

So important is the position of goalkeeper, so unique are her duties compared with those of the other players, that special discussion and treatment concerning her are warranted. She alone can make or break the morale of her team. In a crisis, her decision often decrees the outcome of the game.

FIGURE 17. *Goaltending position*—Goalkeeper with stick in right hand, knees bent, and eyes on the ball, anticipating shot at goal.

As the ball approaches the goalkeeper, she faces it squarely, feet and legs together, in a position about a foot out from the goal line in order to be sure to stop the ball before it crosses the goal line. She changes her position as the ball shifts in the area. She may stop the ball with her hand, stick, instep, or both legs. In the latter instance, she bends her knees and keeps her legs together and her weight forward. If she jumps toward the ball and her legs are straight, the ball will bounce too far away for her to clear it; if she awaits the ball with her legs bent, the ball will drop close in front and be within her reach to drive out to the sides. Running toward the ball to stop it with one foot is not recommended; if the ball is blocked, the goaler is off balance and in an awkward position to clear, and if the goaler misjudges her kick, the ball will go between her legs and probably into the goal. If possible, she keeps the rear (far) corner goal covered with her legs (pads) since the forward driving for goal usually aims at the corners of the goal. She holds her stick low and away from her body, preferably in her right hand. As she kicks, she slides her foot along the ground and kicks with the inside of her instep, knee slightly bent. If she raises her foot she may kick over the ball; if she uses her toe she not only reduces the amount of kicking surface but also takes the chance of raising the ball in the air. Instead of kicking blindly into the attacking forwards, the goaler glances up to select an opening in the forward line to reduce her chances of setting up a return drive for the oncoming attack. A goalkeeper is not penalized if, in stopping a flick, scoop, or raised hit with her hand, the ball rebounds and does not fall perpendicularly to the ground. She is penalized, though, if she bats a raised ball away with her hand.

Although the quickest way for the goaler to remove the ball from the striking region is by kicking, she often uses her stick to clear with a drive to the left or right. For safety's sake, it is best that she not hit the ball on the fly with the stick. If the goaler does not try to stop an attacker's hard drive for goal before she clears it from the mouth of the goal, she may lift the ball off the ground into an attacking player. Whether the clear be by kick or by stick, it should be practically parallel to the end line on the nearer side (Diagram 6). Anytime a goaler clears across the mouth of the goal or into the center of the circle, she drives the ball into the attack and puts her own team at a disadvantage.

Diagram 37 illustrates the position of the goalkeeper as attackers shoot for goal from various angles and close to the goal mouth. In the diagram the mouth of the goal is enlarged to better illustrate the goaler's position in relation to the path of the ball, the opposing forward, and the farther goalpost. The striking circle is not essential to these illustrations; the forward who is attempting to score is about 4 or 5 yards from the goal line. The drawings show an attacker shooting for goal. Assume that she has just either (1) rushed a teammate's drive or her own drive for goal from the edge of the circle (which drive the defense member stopped and hit into the scoring area) or (2) has picked up a pass close to the goal mouth. Backfield players and other opposing line members are omitted from the drawings in order to clarify the goaler's and attacker's positions.

In the drawings the dotted line from the ball to the rear corner of the cage shows that the goaler is in the best position to protect the mouth of the goal. Her legs can block a shot directed to a corner of the goal mouth if the ball approaches from either side. Except in the top illustration, the dotted line from the ball to the rear corner of the cage shows that if the goaler places herself in that direct line she is in the best position to block the shot for goal. The

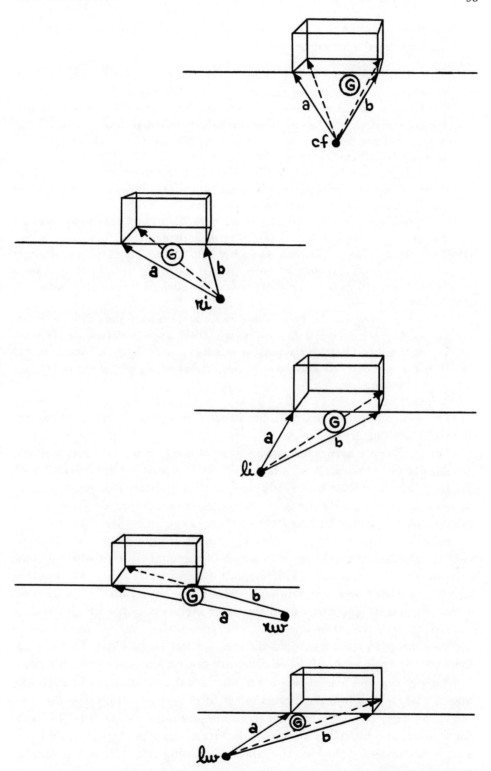

DIAGRAM 37. *Goalkeeper and attackers on close shots for goal mouth.*

solid lines indicate the best possibilities for scoring. The situations pictured in Diagram 37 are described below:

1. Center forward has the ball in front of the goal. She may shoot to either corner. G has placed herself nearer the left side of the goal so that she has less space to cover on her nonstick side. She cannot line herself up with either rear corner of the cage and the ball (note dotted lines) when the ball approaches her from the center. G uses her legs (feet) or stick on drive "a"; uses legs or left foot alone on "b."

2. Right inner has the ball, G on her left. Right inner may drive to either corner. G uses her legs (feet) or stick on "a"; uses both legs or left foot alone on "b." She keeps her weight on the right foot.

3. Left inner has the ball, G on her right. Left inner may shoot to either corner. G uses her legs or stick on "a"; uses both legs or left foot alone on "b."

4. Right wing has the ball, G on her left. Right wing may drive to either corner. G stands close to the nearer post. If the angle is very acute, G keeps her left leg pad next to the post. G uses her stick or feet on "a"; uses both feet on "b."

5. Left wing has the ball, G on her right. Left wing may drive to either corner. G stands close to the nearer post. If the angle is very acute, G keeps her right leg pad next to the post. G uses legs and stick on "a" and both legs or left foot on "b." G may have to rely on her stick alone if she cannot get to the post in time.

The goaler stops the ball with her hand if, in any of the above situations, the ball comes at her in the air.

The goalkeeper *always* remains in front of the goal if there is at least one defense player in the circle with her, or if two forwards are approaching with the ball and the goaler is the only defense player there. If a goaler's teammate misses a tackle near the goal, the goaler always rushes the forward with the ball who is attempting to score at close range.

Experience and the ability to make a quick decision help a goaler to decide whether or not to leave the mouth of the goal. In two situations she *always* comes out to tackle: (1) if she and a forward are practically equidistant from the ball and both must run toward it to get it and (2) if a lone forward who has broken away from the other members of her line is carrying the ball toward the circle and the goalkeeper is the lone defense player in the circle area. In these situations she uses her feet for tackling. This is a safe method; an opponent will have difficulty dodging around the wide pads.

Many goalers are fearful of going out toward the circle edge to meet a lone attacker when they find themselves to be the only defense player in the striking circle. They fail to realize that by coming far out they not only disconcert the forward and hurry her shot from the circle edge but also cut out the possibility of scoring by blocking the attacker's passing area and obstructing her view of the cage.

Diagram 38, a schematic diagram, prepared somewhat to scale, helps picture this situation and illustrates the contention that when a goaltender completely covers the angle formed by the attacker and the two goal posts, she has obliterated the attacker's passing area to the goal as well as blocked her view of the cage. For the purpose of illustration the stationary width of the goaler is assumed to be 2 feet. Her "width" is shown as the white "lane" from the goal mouth out toward the attacker. If the attacker is at points 1, 2, or 3 in the diagram the best position for the goalkeeper to block the passing area (the shaded area open to the attacker to get the ball by the goaler) is at points *a*. (Her "width" covers the angle formed by the attacker and the posts.) Therefore, if an attacker approaches the striking circle alone, the goaler, when she is the *lone defense member* in the circle, can come away from her goal as far as points *a* and effectively protect the entire mouth of the goal, assuming that the attacker with the ball has reached the edge of the circle. Of course, if the goaler can cover effectively more than the assumed width of 2 feet, it follows that she might not have to come out as far as points *a*.

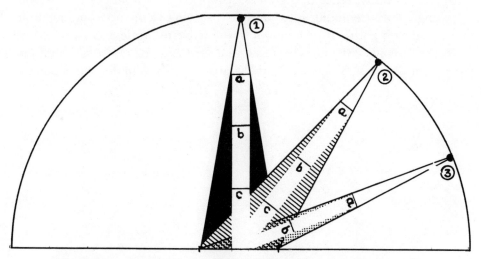

DIAGRAM 38. *Schematic diagram of lone attacker and defender in the striking circle.* (White "lanes" represent paths of goalkeeper. Shaded areas within triangles show passing areas available to forward for shots for goal.)

The diagram proves that when the goalkeeper comes out only as far as positions *b* or *c* (or any spot between points *a* and the goal mouth), sufficient passing area remains open to the attacker to get the ball by the goaler and score. The diagram also shows that an attacker has a greater passing area if she approaches the goal from the center of the striking circle. The nearer the attacker is to the goal line to the right or left of the center, the lesser are her chances to make a goal, since the angle formed by the attacker and the goal posts, and thus the passing area, is considerably reduced.

Naturally, a hard hit from the edge of the circle can be fielded by a goaler who remains in front of the goal. The ball has 15 yards to go; a goaler has time to get in position behind the drive. No one can say that the goaler will field it well and place it accurately for a clear—all before the forward who is rushing the shot reaches the ball. The chances are that the forward will pick up a rebound from the goaler's legs or stick. On the other hand, no forward *should* shoot from the edge of the circle when she is the lone attacker and the goaler the only defender; she dribbles in until the goaler tackles. The attacker should be aware of the fact that a hard hit from the edge of the circle is easier to field than a hard hit from the middle of that area. The goaltender must realize that the longer she waits, the more easily the forward can score, because the goaler has no chance to block an attacker's view of the goal or hurry her shot and has a larger area of the goal mouth to protect. Of course, in any goaltending situation these important conditions are variable and cannot be controlled: the judgment and agility of the goaler, the stick technique of goaler and attacker, the speed of the attacker and the ball, the condition of the field.

Practice in bullying; stopping flicks, scoops, and hard and soft shots from every angle with the hand, stick, and feet; driving to the opposite side from an original stop position; rushing out in the circle to tackle and backing into the goal to avoid obstruction are essential for good goalkeeping technique. More often than not, a mistake by the goaler means a score for the opponent.

Chapter X

Umpiring Technique

by May E. Parry

Umpires are provided to make the game more enjoyable for the players. They are there to see that the spirit of the game is maintained and to create an atmosphere of friendliness and good sportsmanship. The rules of hockey have been made to ensure a game of speed and skill, but unless these rules are properly enforced the skilled players will be hampered by the fouling or roughness of the unskilled.

Umpires must have a thorough knowledge of the rules. They must be decisive in their actions so that they gain the confidence of the players. Umpires must keep up to date on all matters pertaining to hockey by reading the latest publications, attending clinics on umpiring, and discussing controversial points with other umpires.

PERSONAL EQUIPMENT

An umpire must have a loud, clear-toned whistle which is on a cord hung around the neck to prevent dropping or misplacing it. She should also have with her a copy of the current rules and a coin which can be tossed when teams choose ends. An umpire wears suitable clothes which give her complete freedom of movement and which are of a color easily distinguished from that of either team. She usually wears a white blazer or jacket, a skirt that allows easy running, and low flat heeled shoes. She also has a visor cap or sun glasses to protect her eyes against the glare of the sun. Unless an umpire is properly clothed she will not be comfortable and at ease and she will be unable to give the game her undivided attention.

BEFORE THE GAME

An umpire arrives at the field at least fifteen minutes before the game is scheduled to begin. She meets the other umpire and establishes friendly relations with her. The two umpires then decide:

1. Which side of the field each one will take. An umpire standing on the 50-yard line facing the opposite side of the field is responsible for the half of the field to her right. Each umpire makes out-of-bounds decisions the entire length of her side line, and each one calls any fouls occurring near this side line which would be difficult for the other umpire to see.

2. How to handle center bullies. The umpire nearer to the timers takes the opening bully for each half. Then one umpire takes all the center bullies

for the first half of the game and the other umpire takes all the center bullies for the second half.

3. Who will recognize substitutes. The umpire nearer the timers and scorers recognizes substitutes and sends them in at the proper time.

The two umpires then check the playing field and equipment. If there are no goal nets or if there are any holes in the goal nets, then goal umpires are appointed who indicate when the ball has gone into the goal. There should be two goal umpires at each end if it is necessary to provide them. If a field is not properly marked it is tactfully brought to the attention of the captain or coach. The marking of the circle is especially important. If teams have uniforms of a similar color the umpires request that pinnies be worn by one of the teams.

The umpires introduce the two captains and have them choose ends. The captains agree on the length of halves and the length of time between halves. The captains also indicate the goalkeepers for their respective teams. The umpires instruct the captains about substitutions. Substitutes report to the scorers and the nearer umpire who will recognize substitutes.

The umpires check with the timers and scorers. They see that the timers and scorers understand their duties and that they sit together away from the spectators. Scorers should have the correct lineups in their score books, and they should be told to notify the umpire if substitutes enter the game without reporting. The timers should have a clock or watch with a second hand and a second timepiece for use during timeouts. They should also have a horn and, during the last thirty seconds of each half, they should follow the nearer umpire up and down the field so she will know the exact moment when the half ends.

POSITIONING

One of the main factors which will help to make a good umpire is correct positioning. An umpire generally moves up and down the side line about a yard outside the field of play so that all players will be in front of her. There are times, however, when it is absolutely necessary for the umpire to go into the field of play. In order to get a better view of the play when the ball moves into her circle an umpire comes well in, even to the edge of the circle, or behind the goal line. When the play is on the far side of the field, the umpire closes in, but if the play shifts to her side she must not get caught with the right wing behind her. When the ball is in the other half of the field, she does not go past the center line because she must be ready to judge offside if the ball is suddenly returned to her half of the field.

For free hits the umpire stands opposite the spot where the hit is to be taken. When the ball has been placed in the correct position for the hit she anticipates the play and moves ahead in the direction in which the hit is to be taken. On a roll-in she gets into a position so she can see whether the roll-in is taken correctly.

When a corner or penalty corner hit is taken on the far side of the field, the umpire moves in to see the play clearly. When the corner hit is taken on the nearer side of the field, the umpire stays well out until the hit is made and then moves according to the play that follows. During corners and penalty corners the other umpire assists by seeing that the defending forwards stay beyond the 25-yard line, until the ball has been touched by a player other than the one taking the corner hit or until it has come out of the circle.

For center, 25-yard line, and other bullies (except the penalty bully), the umpire takes her position on the goal side of where the bully is being taken. This will enable her to view the bully from a slight angle and will give her an unobstructed view. For a penalty bully the umpire's position must be on the field so that she can clearly see the play without in any way interfering with the two players involved.

When the ball is in the other half of the field, the umpire remains at the center line until there are three defense players in her half of the field or until a forward with the ball in her possession crosses the center line. If there are less than three of the defending team in their own half of the field, any of the attacking forwards who cross the center line without the ball will be offside and the umpire blows her whistle if the ball is hit to any one of them. The free hit is taken from the spot where the offside occurred.

The umpire must be very certain that her decision is correct. Whether or not a player is offside depends upon where she was when the ball was hit to her. A forward who uses her speed and crosses the center line after the ball was hit may appear to be offside by the time she reaches the ball. Many a good player has been wrongly penalized because an umpire either failed to concentrate or did not understand the offside rule. Too many umpires notice only a player's position when she receives a ball instead of noting it when the ball is hit to her. This is an unnecessary mistake that can always be avoided by an umpire who clearly understands the offside rule, who is properly concentrating on the game, and who has placed herself in the correct position.

An umpire must learn from the beginning that there is only one position from which she can correctly see to make offside decisions, and it is up to her to know where that position is and see that she is there. This place to be to see offsides is constantly moving and so, of course, is the umpire. When the umpire positions herself on a line with the third defense player from the goal, she knows that if the ball is on her left any forwards on her right are offside. She must be very observant, however, because the defense players are constantly on the move and a different player may suddenly become the third defense.

When a forward with the ball leaves the third defense player behind and there are only two defense players between her and the goal, then the umpire should keep level with or slightly ahead of the ball. This is the only way she can be sure of who is in front of the ball and who is behind it when it is hit. She must be extremely careful about this because players who are very quick off the mark can move onto the ball with great speed. Unless she is certain where they are when the ball is hit she cannot make the correct decision. The umpire must be constantly aware of any forwards who are offside, but she does not blow her whistle unless the ball is hit towards one of them or unless they are gaining any advantage by being offside. Forwards who are offside when the ball moves into the circle nearly always gain an advantage because the goalkeeper is prevented from giving close concentration to the ball.

If the ball is cleared by the defense and goes into the other half of the field, the umpire should remain in line with the third defense until that player crosses the center line. Forwards are often slow in getting back, and, if they are left in an offside position, the umpire must remain in a position to know which ones are offside. It is better to miss some minor infraction at midfield than to miss an offside which might result in a goal.

SIGNALLING

An umpire blows a short, sharp blast on the whistle to start play, when fouls are made, when the ball goes out of bounds, and to stop play. One long blast is used to indicate half time or the scoring of a goal. A series of short blasts is used when the first whistle blast has not been heard. No whistle is necessary for a 25-yard line bully, for a free hit, a corner hit, or a roll-in to be taken.

After blowing for a foul or a roll-in, an umpire signals with one arm raised sideways to shoulder height and pointing in the direction the hit or roll-in is to be taken. If players do not know where to place the ball on a free hit, it is better to indicate this by using the voice.   If it is necessary to point to the spot, the arm indicating the direction of the free hit should be lowered because two arm signals are often confusing.

On a roll-in the whistle, the arm signal, and the voice are all used. The arm signal can be seen by players at a distance, and will help speed up play.

It is well to remember that players are accustomed to the simple method of one arm pointing at shoulder height in the direction of the free hit or roll-in, so it is best to be orthodox, to eliminate all unnecessary movements, and to resist any tendency to acquire original mannerisms.

HOLDING THE WHISTLE

At the beginning of a game, umpires should be strict and give close attention to detail. Then, if the game is well under control, they should hold the whistle as much as possible and allow the game to flow.

A good umpire soon learns to hold her whistle to the advantage of the team that has been fouled. After a foul has been committed, an umpire waits long enough to see which team gains the advantage and blows the whistle only if the advantage goes to the side which fouled. When the defense fouls in the circle, the umpire must be especially careful not to blow too quickly because there is nothing more aggravating to a forward who is ready to shoot for goal.

If rough play is not penalized because the umpire is holding her whistle, a warning should be given to the offending player. If a forward is given her chance to score but fails to do so, she should not then have a free hit or penalty corner awarded to her as well. This would be a double penalty for a foul.

BULLIES, CORNERS, FREE HITS, ROLL-INS

The following points are to be noted on bullies:

1. All players must be onside until the bully is complete.
2. The two players taking the bully must stand squarely facing the side lines and must not move their feet until the bully is complete.
3. No other player may be nearer than 5 yards until the bully is complete.
4. Only the flat side of the stick may be used for making contact with the opponent's stick, and sticks must hit three times before the bully is complete.
5. One of the two players bullying must hit the ball before it is in play.
6. The ball must be correctly placed when the bully is taken. If on the 25-yard line, it should be opposite the spot where it went out. If bullied after a double foul, it should be on the spot where the breach occurred but not nearer than 5 yards from the goal. When the ball goes over the side line off the sticks of two opponents, it should be bullied on the 5-yard line by the opposing wings.
7. For any breach of the bully rule the bully shall be taken again.

The following points are to be noted on corners:

1. A long corner is awarded when the ball glances off a defense player and goes over the goal line not between the goal posts, or when the ball is hit by an attacker outside the striking circle and it is then hit by or glances off a defender into the goal. A penalty or short corner is awarded when a defense player intentionally hits the ball over the goal line not between the goal posts, or when a defense player fouls inside the striking circle.
2. Six of the defending team must have feet and sticks behind the goal line until the corner hit has been taken. For a violation of this rule the corner hit is taken again. However, this is a good time for the umpire to hold her whistle if the corner is well hit because the forward may be able to get her shot off.
3. The defending forwards must remain beyond the nearer 25-yard line until the ball has been touched by a player other than the one taking the corner hit, or until the ball has gone out of the striking circle.
4. The attacking team must have both feet and sticks outside the striking circle until the ball has been hit.
5. Forwards may not shoot for goal unless the ball has been stopped, not necessarily motionless, or unless the ball has touched the stick or person of one of the defending team.
6. The ball must be placed in the correct position. A long corner is taken on the goal or side line within 5 yards of the corner on the side of the field

where the ball went out. If the ball goes into the goal and a corner is awarded, the attacking team may choose the side from which the corner hit is taken. A penalty corner is taken from a point on the goal line not less than 10 yards from the nearer goal post on either side of the field according to the choice of the attacking team.

7. All other players must be at least 5 yards away from the player taking the corner hit.
8. The player taking the corner hit may stand with her feet in any position. She must not make sticks, hit the ball a second time until it has been touched by another player, or remain in an offside position after the hit. If she fouls, the defense is given a free hit which may be taken anywhere in the circle or on the spot where the foul occurred.

The following points are to be noted on free hits:

1. The free hit is taken on the spot where the foul occurred. The umpire should not be too fussy about this if the ball is placed in the approximate position and no advantage is being gained. It is often difficult when a player is being called for offside and her position is some distance from the ball. The rule states that the free hit is to be taken where the foul occurred and umpires should be more strict about this.
2. All other players must be at least 5 yards away from the player taking the free hit. If the player taking the hit prefers to take it quickly rather than wait for an opponent to move farther away, she should be allowed to do so, unless she is sending it to one of her own team who is also too close.
3. The ball must be motionless when the free hit is taken.
4. The player taking the hit must not make sticks and she must not hit it a second time until it has been touched by another player.

For violation of points 1 or 2 the free hit is taken again. For violation of points 3 or 4 a free hit is given to the other side. If the player taking the free hit misses the ball completely, she may take the hit again provided she has not made sticks.

The following points are to be noted on roll-ins:

1. The ball must be rolled so that it touches the ground in the field of play within 1 yard of where it went out.
2. The ball must be rolled not bounced or spun.
3. The player taking the roll-in must have feet and stick behind the side line until the ball leaves her hand.
4. All other players must be beyond the 5-yard line in the field of play until the ball is rolled in.

For any breach of the rule by the player taking the roll-in, the roll-in is taken by a player of the opposite team. If the player takes the roll-in without her stick in her hand, a free hit in the alley is given to the other team. If, on an attempted roll-in, the ball does not enter the field of play the roll-in is taken again. For any breach of the rules by any other player, the roll-in is taken again.

PENALTY BULLY

A penalty bully is awarded for a wilful breach of a rule, for repeated fouling, or for any foul which prevents a goal from being scored. When a penalty bully is called it is usually against the goalkeeper, but it may also be called against any of the defense. The following are some examples:

1. If the goalkeeper falls down and makes no effort to get up again, thus blocking the goal with her body and preventing the forwards from scoring.
2. If a goalkeeper or a defense player stops a shot at goal by using the wrong side of the stick or lifts the blade of the stick to stop a scoop shot at goal.
3. If the goalkeeper stops the ball with her feet and then keeps the ball trapped under her feet to prevent the forwards from getting another shot.

The bully is taken on a spot 5 yards in front of the center of the goal line by the player who fouled and any player chosen by the attacking team. All other players must remain beyond the nearer 25-yard line until the bully has been completed. The umpire starts and ends the bully by her whistle, and she stands so that she can see that neither player fouls. If the defender is the goalkeeper, she loses her two special privileges of kicking and of being able to have the ball rebound from her open hand. (The goalkeeper also loses these privileges when she is outside the striking circle.) The goalkeeper may not take time to remove her pads if she is taking part in a penalty bully. Extra time is allowed if half-time or time is called before a penalty bully has been completed.

A goal is scored and play is restarted on the center line if

1. The ball goes into the goal off either player.
2. The defender fouls.

The penalty bully is taken again if

1. The defender sends the ball over the goal line not between the goal posts.
2. There is a double foul or an improper bully.
3. Any other player interferes.
4. The ball goes over the goal line not between the goal posts off the sticks of both players.

The bully is over and play is restarted at the center of the 25-yard line if

1. The attacker fouls.
2. The attacker sends the ball over the goal line not between the goal posts.
3. The defender sends the ball outside the circle into the field of play.

FOULS

It is very important for an umpire to call anything dangerous or likely to lead to dangerous play. Roughness and wild hitting seriously spoil the spirit of the game and can easily result in an accident. Often a word of caution from an umpire early in the game is all that is needed to prevent anything of this kind from developing.

STICKS

No part of the stick, blade or handle, may be raised above the shoulder when playing the ball. If umpires are strict about calling sticks at the beginning of the game, players will see that they keep their sticks down.

KICKING AND ADVANCING

The ball may not be moved in any direction except by the stick; so, if it rebounds off the foot, leg, body, or hand of a player she should be penalized. If there is a kick in the circle by the defense, the umpire holds her whistle until she can see who plays the ball. Frequently a forward can get on to the ball and shoot for goal—and she prefers this to having a penalty corner awarded. The umpire must decide quickly about this, for, once she has let the forward have her chance to score, she cannot change her mind if the forward shoots wide or makes a poor hit.

If the ball is in the air, the sooner it is brought down the better—and players should be encouraged to use their hands for this purpose. The ball must be released immediately, and fall to the ground without being placed in any direction.

Advancing is not called on a player when the ball is hit directly into her by an opponent at close range. This is dangerous hitting and the player who made the hit should be penalized. Neither is advancing called on a player when the ball hits her heel causing her to stop and go back to recover the ball. If the ball glances off her heel advantageously, or if she obstructs when she recovers the ball, then it is a foul. A ball that hits a player's leg or foot and does not advance is not a foul.

DANGEROUS PLAY

Undercutting the ball, hitting at an oncoming ball without first controlling it, hitting into an opponent, goalie clears which rise dangerously, and balls scooped into a crowd of players all come under this heading.

Undercutting is hitting at the ball with the blade of the stick laid back, thus causing the ball to rise. It is usually done by a player hitting with her weight too far back or hitting when too far from the ball. The umpire can usually see when this occurs and she should call it instantly, instead of waiting to see where the ball goes. If a forward is shooting for goal, it is much better to call the foul the moment the ball leaves the forward's stick rather than to call it after the ball has gone into the goal.

Dangerous hitting should always be called. Any player who hits at a ball coming straight towards her without stopping or controlling it is apt to make the ball rise if she hits it back in the direction from which it came. Not only may some one be injured, but, because of this dangerous type of play, opponents will be afraid to move in on this player. A goalkeeper who kicks the ball into the air is gaining a tremendous advantage because the forwards will be afraid to rush her also. Rough play should never be permitted, and the umpire should always call it the moment it occurs. A game that tends to be rough will very quickly improve if the umpires are firm in calling any form of dangerous play. A player may be suspended from the game for rough play or misconduct.

INTERFERENCE WITH STICKS

This happens most often on misjudged tackles, and it results in a player hitting an opponent's stick instead of the ball. It may occur on left-hand lunges or on reverse stick tackles, and, even though the player may continue with the ball, she may have been hampered enough so that a foul is called. When a player tackles with only one hand on her stick, the accuracy and control of her movements should be watched. She must be very accurate to play the ball and not interfere with her opponent in any way. When this foul occurs in midfield, it should usually be called because it will make the players more conscious of the fact that it is not a legal play. When the defense makes this foul in the circle, the umpire holds her whistle until she can see the resulting play.

OBSTRUCTION

A player is not allowed to interpose herself in any way as an obstruction. She may not obstruct her opponent by running in between her and the ball or by using her feet or any part of her body to prevent her opponent from playing the ball. A forward with the ball who is moving straight for goal will not obstruct if she continues doing just that. If an opponent comes up on one side of her and she uses her body to prevent the opponent from playing the ball, then she is obstructing. A forward may often be seen putting the ball on the far side of her pursuer and shielding the ball with her body. This is definitely a foul and should be called. The reverse tackle may result in obstruction because the player making the tackle may hit the opponent's stick, she may trip her up, or she may interpose her shoulder so that she impedes the progress of the player. Any of these actions is a foul.

A forward who is closely marked and who turns in a circle towards her own goal line when receiving the ball always obstructs. If there is no one within playing distance of her, then it is not a foul. Some umpires seem to consider any use of the reverse stick a foul, but it is only a foul if the player obstructs in any way due to the use of the reverse stick.

Another form of obstruction is one which is not called often enough. This occurs when one defense obstructs and another defense plays the ball. The defense player who gets the ball does not foul, but a foul is called because of the first player's actions.

OFFSIDE

A player will not be offside if she is in her own half of the field, if she is behind the ball, or if she has three of her opponents nearer their own goal

line than she is at the moment the ball is hit or rolled into her by one of
her own side. The most difficult time to see offside is when the play is in the
circle. Here the pace quickens, play is more concentrated, and it is difficult
to watch both the attacking forward line and the ball. Any missed offside
here may result in a goal, so an umpire must be especially vigilant.

Umpires must remember that the actions of the opposing defense cannot
put an offside player onside. If a third defense player moves between an offside player and the goal, this does not put her onside. She can, however, in
this position be put onside by having the ball hit to her by one of her own
team who is onside.

OTHER FOULS

No personal contact is allowed in hockey, and any player who pushes or
charges into another player should immediately be whistled up. Rough play
in any form should never be condoned.

The rounded side of the stick may not be used for hitting or stopping. A
player may not take part in the game unless she has her stick in her hand.
If a player drops her stick, the umpire should know whether this was acci-
dental or whether it was knocked out of her hand by rough or careless play.
If the goalkeeper drops her stick and plays without it, a penalty bully may
be called against her. If she stops the ball successfully, then drops her stick
while clearing, a penalty corner should be called.

OTHER ESSENTIAL POINTS

GOAL SCORING

To score a goal the umpire must be sure the whole ball goes entirely over
the goal line under the crossbar. The ball must have been hit by or glanced
off the stick of an attacker while the ball was in the striking circle. If the ball
is hit by an attacker outside the circle and it goes into the goal, it is a 25-
yard bully, unless it touched a defense player on the way, in which case a
corner is the correct decision.

ACCIDENTS AND INTERFERENCE WITH THE GAME

If a player is injured, the game is stopped but not for more than five
minutes at any one time. Play may also be stopped if a player breaks her stick
and cannot quickly be supplied with another one. Play is resumed by a
bully unless a roll-in, corner, penalty corner, penalty bully, free hit, or 25-
yard bully has been awarded. The ball is bullied on a spot chosen by the
umpire in whose half of the field the accident occurred.

If the ball hits an umpire or any obstruction, it is considered in play unless it goes off the field, or would have gone off if the interference had not
occurred. In this case the usual rule for out-of-bounds play is followed.

If the ball becomes lodged in the goalkeeper's pads or in the clothing of a player, a bully is taken on the spot but not less than 5 yards from the goal line.

If the umpire feels the game is being interfered with, she may suspend play temporarily until the situation can be dealt with. This covers such things as spectators coming onto the field and interfering with play or dogs straying onto the field.

SUBSTITUTIONS

Substitutes may be put into the game only at half time, in case of accident, or in case of disqualification. Substitutes must report to the scorers and be authorized by the umpire designated to recognize substitutes. In school or college games, if coaches agree, substitution may be made at a bully or corner. For breach of this rule a penalty corner is awarded to the opposing team. For simultaneous breach of the rule by both teams the game is stopped when the ball is dead. Players are notified of the infringement, and play is restarted by a bully.

WRONG DECISIONS

If the ball goes over the goal line and the umpire calls a 25-yard line bully but a defense player says she touched the ball last, the umpire should change her decision and award a corner. If an umpire gives a free hit in the wrong direction but realizes her mistake before the penalty is taken, she should change her decision. If the umpire blows her whistle when she should have held it, she should enforce the penalty. Play has stopped and the advantage has been lost, so the umpire must stick to her decision in this case.

SOME UMPIRING DO'S AND DON'TS

Do	Don't
1. Cooperate with the players and with the other umpire. Have a pleasant and friendly manner.	1. Be officious and call fouls in the other half of the field except near your side line.
2. Let the game move along whenever possible. Keep yourself as inconspicuous as possible.	2. Take the game away from the players. It belongs to them and not to the umpires.
3. Make your arm signals as quickly as possible after calling a foul.	3. Use unnecessary arm movements and don't use both arms in signalling.
4. Have confidence in your ability to control the game.	4. Be indecisive and hesitant even if you feel that way.
5. Keep at least 1 yard outside the field of play as the ball moves in your half of the field.	5. Get drawn into the alley and be in the player's way because the wings and wing halves need room to play.

Do

6. Come into the field of play when the ball moves into your circle so you can see what is happening.

7. Know the offside rule and know where the forwards are when the ball is hit to them.

8. Always penalize dangerous play. This includes dangerous kicking by the goalkeeper.

9. Learn to recognize all types of obstruction. Call it when one player obstructs and another plays it.

10. Hold the whistle if the team fouled against gains the advantage.

11. Know your rules thoroughly and be prepared in case the unexpected should happen.

12. Practice as much as possible and listen to friendly criticism. This will make you a better umpire.

Don't

6. Get caught with the right wing behind you because you will be in the way and you won't know if she is offside.

7. Concentrate so much on the ball that you miss an offside or call one incorrectly.

8. Let the goalkeeper clear the ball into the air because the forwards will be afraid to rush her.

9. Call obstruction on a player who turns with the ball when no one is near enough to her to play the ball.

10. Blow too quickly when the defense fouls in the circle.

11. Hesitate in making your decisions. You must know the correct answer and be decisive about it.

12. Be satisfied with your umpiring or you may become careless. You can learn a great deal from watching others.

GLOSSARY OF FIELD HOCKEY TERMS

EQUIPMENT

Blade—the curved end of the stick (see also Head).

Composition ball—an inexpensive cork ball of regulation weight for stickwork.

Dress—distinctive uniforms worn by members of a team and by officials.

Face—the flat side of the blade.

Goal cage—a 12-foot wide, 7-foot high, and 4- to 6-foot deep opening made of beams and posts, enclosed on the sides, back, and top with nets.

Goalie shoes—heavy, well-padded leather shoes with leather cleats.

Grip—a 15- to 18-inch covering, usually of rubber, for the handle of the stick.

Head—the blade of the stick.

Insertions or inserts—strips of rubber spliced into the length of the cane handle to permit flexibility of the handle and to absorb shock when the stick hits the ball.

Kicking pads—canvas protectors for the goalkeeper's toes and insteps.

Lime—a commercially prepared white powder used to line the hockey field.

Marker—a machine or brush for putting the regulation lines on the field.

Match ball—a 5½-ounce to 5¾-ounce white ball made of leather, cork, and twine or of plastic.

Pads—canvas protections for the legs, shins, and insteps.

Pinnies—colored vest-like garments worn by players to distinguish teams.

Shin guards—see Pads.

Shoes—special canvas shoes with rubber cleats molded to rubber soles, or leather shoes with leather bars on the soles.

Sponge—thick, soft rubber for use in the goaler's shoes as shock absorbers.

Stick or hockey stick—an implement, with a narrow handle and a curved blade with flat surface on its left side only, which is used to hit the ball.

Stubs—pieces of wood or iron, driven flush with the ground at the boundary corners and sections of the field to facilitate relining.

Toe—the end of the blade of the stick.

FIELD

Alley lines—broken lines inside the side boundaries of the field, extending between the two goal lines, parallel to and 5 yards from the side lines.

Alleys—two lanes, 5 yards wide, on either side of the hockey field between the two goal lines, bounded on the outside by the side lines and on the inside by the 5-yard lines.

Boundary lines—the side lines and goal lines.

Center line—the middle line, parallel to the goal lines, which divides the field into two equal parts.

Five-yard lines—see Alley lines.

Five-yard mark—a spot on both the goal lines and the side lines, 5 yards out from each corner of the field, which is used for a corner hit.

Out of bounds—outside the goal or side lines.

Side lines—boundary lines extending the length of the field (90 to 100 yards).

Striking circle—a space enclosed by two quarter circles, each with a radius of 15 yards, drawn from the goal line with each goal post as a center, joined by a 4-yard line parallel to the goal mouth.

Ten-yard mark—a spot on the goal line, 10 yards out from each goal post, which is used for a penalty corner.

Twenty-five-yard lines—two lines extending between the side lines, parallel to and 25 yards from the goal lines.

GENERAL

Advancing—moving the ball to an advantageous position with any part of the body; a foul.

Backing up—staying close behind a teammate who has the ball; staying close behind a teammate who is tackling an opponent.

Being left behind—being of no defensive assistance; being passed by an opponent following an unsuccessful tackle.

Bully—the technique used to start or restart the game when a player from each team has an equal opportunity to get the ball.

Carrying the ball—propelling the ball with the stick by means of short taps.

Centering the ball—passing it toward the striking circle from the side area of the field.

Charging—playing with the weight uncontrolled and the head down, resulting in a collision with an opponent; a foul.

Checking the speed—slowing up.

Clearing—driving the ball from a congested area; kicking the ball out of scoring range (goalkeeper only).

Corner—a hit awarded a member of the attacking team whenever a member of the defense unintentionally hits the ball out of play over the goal line (not between the posts); a hit by an attacker taken on a spot 5 yards from a corner of the field, on the goal line or side line.

Covering—playing deeply. A safety measure used by defense players on the side of the field away from the ball; by playing deeply they are able to intercept long passes and to shift to mark or tackle players whose defense has been left behind.

Deflecting—changing the direction of the ball with the stick, without first stopping the ball.

Distributing the play—changing the direction of the ball so that players on either side of the field have an equal amount of play; dividing active play among all players.

Dodging—getting by an opponent, still keeping possession of the ball; passing within a small area in such a manner that the passer evades the opponent and picks up the ball.

Dribbling—carrying the ball at top speed down the field; hitting the ball ahead through a series of stick taps.

Fielding—stopping the ball or changing its direction with the stick, hand, or foot; placing the ball, on an attempted stop, in an advantageous position for playing it again; receiving a pass.

Foul—an infringement of the rules, such as kicking, undercutting, charging, obstructing, hooking, making sticks, playing in an offside position, advancing the ball off the body.

Free hit—an uncontested hit awarded a member of one team as the result of an infringement of the rules by an opponent—a hit with no one permitted nearer to the hitter than 5 yards.

Giving with the stick—relaxing the grip to relieve the tension as the ball hits the stick; pulling back the club with the wrists and arms at the moment the ball meets the stick to lessen the impact and prevent the ball from bounding out of reach.

Goal—one point awarded the team when the ball, hit by or glanced off the stick of an attack player inside the striking circle, passes entirely over the goal line between the posts and under the crossbar.

Going to meet the ball—moving toward an oncoming ball to play it.

Gripping—holding the handle of the stick firmly.

Guarding—see Marking.

Hitting on the fly—hitting an approaching ball without first stopping or fielding it.

Holding the whistle—deferring a decision; delaying to call a foul at the time a player commits the breach of rule until it is determined whether an opponent gets the advantage.

Hooking—using the stick to hold an opponent's stick and keep her out of play; a foul.

Intercepting—picking up a hit to an opponent before a member of the opponent's team can play the ball; taking possession of a ball directed to an opponent.

Interchanging—readjusting one's position on the field to assume a teammate's duties when the teammate is left behind and cannot recover her own position; temporarily exchanging positions.

Kick—the bounce of the ball, to an advantageous position, from the foot of the person stopping the ball; a foul (except by goalkeeper).

Making spaces—drawing an opponent out of the play or out of a certain area (space) so that a teammate with the ball may direct a pass through the space.

Marking—staying about a yard from one's opponent, usually on her stick side; playing close enough to an opponent to prevent her from receiving a pass, or to tackle her the moment she receives the ball; watching an opponent closely.

Marking loosely—playing within 5 or 10 yards of an opponent, on her stick side.

Nonstick side—the left side of a player.

Obstructing—a foul which occurs when one player hinders or prevents her opponent from playing the ball by placing her body or part of her body between that player and the ball.

Offside—being nearer the opponents' goal line than the ball, with less than three opponents between the player and the ball (occurs on the opponents' half of the field); an infringement of the rules.

Overrunning the ball—losing the ball behind oneself through fumbling the dribble or the pass.

Overtaking a player—catching up to an opponent who has the ball.

Passing—directing the ball to a teammate or to a space where a teammate is expected to move; transferring the ball from one player's stick to another's.

Penalty bully—an award to the attacking team for a defenders' breach of a rule when a goal might have been scored by the attack had not the breach of the rule occurred.

Penalty corner—a hit awarded a member of the attacking team if a member of the defense intentionally directs the ball out of play over the goal line (not between the posts) or commits a foul within the striking circle; a hit by an attacker taken on a spot at least 10 yards from the goal post on the goal line.

Penalty goal—a point awarded the attacking team if a defender fouls during a penalty bully.

Picking up a pass—receiving or intercepting the ball and carrying it onward without checking the speed.

Placing the ball—fielding the ball to a player's advantage; relaxing the grip as the impact of the ball on the stick occurs and turning the wrists to put the ball within reaching distance.

Positioning—placing oneself on the field in relation to the ball, to opponents, and to teammates; as umpire, placing oneself in relation to the ball, the players, and the game situation.

Reversing the stick—using the stick with the toe pointing to the ground.

Roll-in—a hand technique employed to put the ball into play after it has gone over the side lines.

Rushing—running toward a player or the goal following a pass or hard drive in the same direction, in an effort to cause the opponent to hurry her play or to get the rebound from the goalie.

Shooting—aiming the ball for goal.

Signaling—raising of the umpire's arm sideways to shoulder height in the direction in which the free hit or roll-in is to be taken.

Standing squarely—standing directly behind a stationary ball, feet astride and parallel, in a position such that the ball and feet form an isosceles triangle.

Steadying the ball—controlling the ball after fielding (stopping) it.

Stick side—the right side of a player.

Sticks—a term used to indicate that a player has raised her stick above shoulder level in the act of hitting or stopping the ball; a foul.

Tackling—meeting an opponent who has the ball with intent to get possession of the ball or force the opponent to pass it.

Tackling back—attempting to recover the ball after missing a tackle by immediately turning back after the opponent with the ball.

Tightening the wrists—locking the grip on the handle of the stick; grasping the handle of the stick firmly.

Timing—accurately judging when to pass the ball, how hard or far to hit it to a teammate; judging the exact moment to tackle an opponent with the ball.

Trapping the ball—stopping the ball by catching it under the foot.

Undercutting—hitting the ball with the stick blade facing up (laid back) so that the ball rises into the air; a foul.

PASSES

Back—a pass to a teammate who is behind the ball-carrier.

Diagonal—a long or short pass on an angle and ahead of a teammate.

Oncoming—a pass moving directly toward a player (usually hit by the opponent).

Square—a pass across to a player who is in line with the ball-carrier.

Through—a drive far ahead, through members of both the defense and offense.

Triangular—a short pass to a teammate who immediately returns the ball.

PERSONS

Attack—a general term for the team in possession of the ball; a general term for the forwards on a team.

Attacking team—the team in possession of the ball.

Backfield players, backs, defense members, defenders—synonymous for the six members in the backfield.

Center forward—the central player among the line members.

Center halfback—the central player among the halfbacks.

Defensive team—the team which does not have the ball.

Defense—a general term for the team not in possession of the ball; a general term for the backfield members of a team.

Forwards, attackers, line players, offensive members—synonymous for the five members on the forward line.

Fullbacks, left and right—defensive members usually playing between the halfbacks and the goalkeeper.

Goalkeeper, goalie, goaler—synonymous for the defensive member guarding the mouth of the goal.

Goal umpire—a judge to assist the official in acknowledging goals scored when the goal cages do not conform to regulations.

Halfbacks, left and right—defensive members usually playing between the line players and the fullbacks.

Home team—the team acting as hostess to another and holding the game on its own field.

Inners (or inside players), left and right—line members maintaining positions between the center forward and the wings.

Offensive team—the team in possession of the ball.

Official—(see Umpire).

Opponent—an opposing player or an opposing team.

Umpire—the person who rules on the plays of the hockey game.

Visiting team—the team invited to meet the home team on the latter's field.

Wings (or outside players), left and right—the outermost members of the forward line.

STROKES

Carry—a method of holding the stick across the body in two hands (or one hand) when not playing the ball.

Circular tackle—a means of overtaking an opponent who is on the right and attempting to secure the ball without obstructing by making a semicircle to the right in front of the opponent and taking the ball at the same time.

Close dribble—a method of propelling the ball with soft taps so that it remains under control near the right foot (see also Dribble, Loose dribble).

Dribble—a two-handed stroke, hands apart, employed most often by the line players for propelling the ball down the field.

Drive—a two-handed hit, hands together, which carries considerable impetus and adapts itself to long distance hitting; used for shooting, clearing, passing.

Flick—a two-handed reaching stroke, hands apart, which raises the ball slightly from the ground, putting spin on it through a twist of the wrists; excellent for shooting for goal.

Job—a one-handed spoiling stroke, a jab at the ball to get it away from an opponent.

Left drive—a two-handed stroke, hands together, used to hit to the left from either foot.

Left-hand lunge—a one-handed, long-reaching stroke used to break up an opponent's progress with the ball.

Loose dribble—a method of propelling the ball with hard taps so that, though controlled, it goes ahead of the dribbler; used when the dribbler has a clear field ahead (see also Dribble, Close dribble).

Push—a two-handed stroke, hands apart, used for short passes and executed without a backswing by scraping the stick along the ground.

Reverse—a two-handed stroke, hands together, performed by turning the handle of the stick in the grasp so that the toe of the stick points toward the ground.

Right cut—a two-handed reversed-stick stroke, hands together, employed when overtaking an opponent on her nonstick side.

Right drive—a two-handed stroke, hands together, used to hit to the right from the right foot.

Right-hand lunge—a one-handed reversed-stick stroke generally employed when overtaking an opponent on her nonstick side.

Scoop—a two-handed reaching stroke, hands apart, which lifts the ball over an opponent's stick; a shovel or lifting stroke.

Index